the language of layout

BUD DONAHUE

Bud Donahue is Associate Professor of Graphic Design,
Louisiana Tech University. He has had over
thirty years experience (in New York, Detroit, Chicago)
as a freelance illustrator, layout artist, art director,
creative director, and owner of his own art studio.

A SPECTRUM BOOK

Prentice-Hall, Inc., *Englewood Cliffs, New Jersey 07632*

Library of Congress Cataloging in Publication Data

DONAHUE, BUD.
   The language of layout.

   (The Art & design series)   (A Spectrum Book)
   1. Advertising layout and typography.
I. Title. II. Series.
HF5825.D65   659.13'24   78-6949
ISBN 0-13-522953-7
ISBN 0-13-522961-8 pbk.

THE ART AND DESIGN SERIES

Printed in the United States of America

10   9   8

To the terrific shirt-sleeve art directors for whom I have worked . . .

To the artists who tolerated and supported me as an art director . . .

To the rough-tough layout artists with whom I have competed, and from whom I have learned . . .

To the writers who made my job easier . . .

To my wife and family, who somehow survived the years of night-and-day assignments . . .

This book is dedicated.

PRENTICE-HALL INTERNATIONAL, INC., *London*
PRENTICE-HALL OF AUSTRALIA PTY. LIMITED, *Sydney*
PRENTICE-HALL OF CANADA, LTD., *Toronto*
PRENTICE-HALL OF INDIA A PRIVATE LIMITED, *New Delhi*
PRENTICE-HALL OF JAPAN, INC., *Tokyo*
PRENTICE-HALL OF SOUTHEAST ASIA PTE. LTD., *Singapore*
WHITEHALL BOOKS LIMITED, *Wellington, New Zealand*

preface

There is nothing revolutionary in this book. No panaceas. There are some guidelines, some ideas, some techniques, and a great deal of affection for the industry in which we participate.

We are experiencing a period of disbelief and distrust resulting from years of jabberwocky dumped upon us by everyone from the federal government down to the late-night TV automobile huckster. The copywriter–layout artist team faces a disenchanted and disinterested audience that can only be swayed by an honest message, imaginatively presented. If this book can help a young layout artist, interest an old pro and nudge a few creative instincts, it will have accomplished its purpose.

My hope is that it will do just that.

All the drawing and display lettering in this book is intended to be LAYOUT rendering. Any resemblance to illustration or finished lettering is strictly coincidental . . . and unintended.

Murphy's First Law:
If anything can go wrong . . . it will.

introduction

A competent layout artist of the forties would be lost in an art department of the seventies. Demands upon graphic communicators for clarity, brevity, and believability have increased manifestly over the last three decades. What sufficed as advertising in the lush shortage years of the forties and early fifties is no longer acceptable. In the forties, demand exceeded supply and merchandisers had little need for the skilled communicator: the language, the symbols of layout were primitive, undeveloped. In the fifties, demand continued to exceed supply, but a small corps of imaginative, highly creative designers broke loose with sparkling new ideas, new graphic symbols, and a host of imitators happily fell in behind them.

The renaissance of communicative design reflected a period of technological growth that equaled or surpassed the Industrial Revolution. · Who in the forties could have predicted an audience so blasé as to complain when television coverage of the moon landing interfered with the soap operas? Or be dissatisfied with the first films from a robot camera on Mars because they were lacking in color?

Who could predict six commercials fighting for attention during every TV station break? Or even predict television as we know it?

What linotype operator would even dream of the phototypesetter with its electronic brain? The computer that learns, remembers, and tells all? And even draws pictures (not very good ones, thank heavens)!

New skills were required and were developed. New professions became a mainstay of all industries and the communications industry, after a slow start, moved to catch up . . . and to deal with soaring costs. Before inflation ever became a really important factor in our lives, costs of time, space, service, and distribution skyrocketed. The greatly expanded circulation of the print media (those which had survived the onslaught of TV) led to spiralling space rates. Added to the steadily increasing demand for the eye and ear of the public, it created a whole new set of values for the communications industry.

The audience became more discriminating, the client more demanding, the ad manager more attentive to his/her homework, and the art director more and more a skilled communicator—a student of the media, a cost-conscious innovator, a demanding interpreter of trends with a mind finely tuned to graphic symbolization.

And right beside the art director sat the layout artist. Not at the bottom of a bureaucratic ladder, but up at the top where the complex activity of graphic communication began. Right next to another whose individual importance had changed little over the years: the copywriter. To this date, no computer, no market researcher, no pollster or statistician has been able to supersede the creative intuition and technical proficiency of the writer-artist combination. Nor have the writer and artist been able to stand still. They have had to learn more, think faster, adapt more easily, and rebound more quickly to survive.

The era of excellence continued through the sixties and into the seventies, when a recession sent advertisers back into their hard-sell, hard-shell, play-it-safe protectiveness. Though the recession ended several years ago, creativity is still struggling to return to layout. There are striking exceptions, exciting graphics. The beginning of a new era of creativity? Perhaps, though the major-ity of today's designs in print just do not communicate.

Oddly, despite this low ebb in print advertising, the demands upon the layout artist for technical proficiency have continued to increase. Today's run-of-the-mill layout is better drawn, better rendered, and could have been better conceived than the comprehensive of thirty years ago if advertisers would stop depending on the BIG Photograph and realize that art (photographs included) and copy are partners, that research and intuition are partners, and that creativity cannot be computerized. Then the writer and the layout artist would again blend their imaginations and their technical skills.

Then there really would be an exciting new era of communication in print.

contents

THE PROBLEM

Your client, through a fault of his own (not admitted, of course), is the possessor of ten million cans of KINKIE, a hair-curling spray. Despite a high-powered nationwide promotion extolling its virtues and promising miraculous results (with one eye on the FTC), the reaction of consumers across the country was a cold and uncompromising "NO SALE."

Quote: It smells to me like rotten wood.

Quote: I detect the definite odor of rusting metal.

For Your File:

1. A loose indication of lettering of your own design is safer than a more comped (comprehensive or finished) rendering, which can end up looking like poor-quality finished art.

2. When rendering cartoons as comped as these, *know your client.* The temptation to use them as illustrations can overpower those who value the buck saved.

OUR CAST OF CHARACTERS, STARTING CLOCKWISE FROM THE LOWER LEFT:

THE CLIENT: HE GOT INTO THE MESS...THE AGENCY SHOULD GET HIM OUT !

THE COPY CHIEF: SHE STAYED UP ALL NIGHT PLANNING THE RESCUE.

THE ACCOUNT EXEC: ALL AMERICAN 1967...GREAT ON THE LONG LUNCH CIRCUIT.

THE COPYWRITER: SHE WAS OUT ALL NIGHT, TOO, BUT NOT ON A RESCUE MISSION.

THE ART DIRECTOR: A GENTLE SOUL WITH ULCERS AND HYPERTENSION...A PILL-POPPER.

DON'T SELL ANY OF THESE PEOPLE SHORT. WE KID ABOUT THEM...WE BATTLE WITH THEM... <u>BUT</u>

WE COULD NOT EXIST WITHOUT THEM!

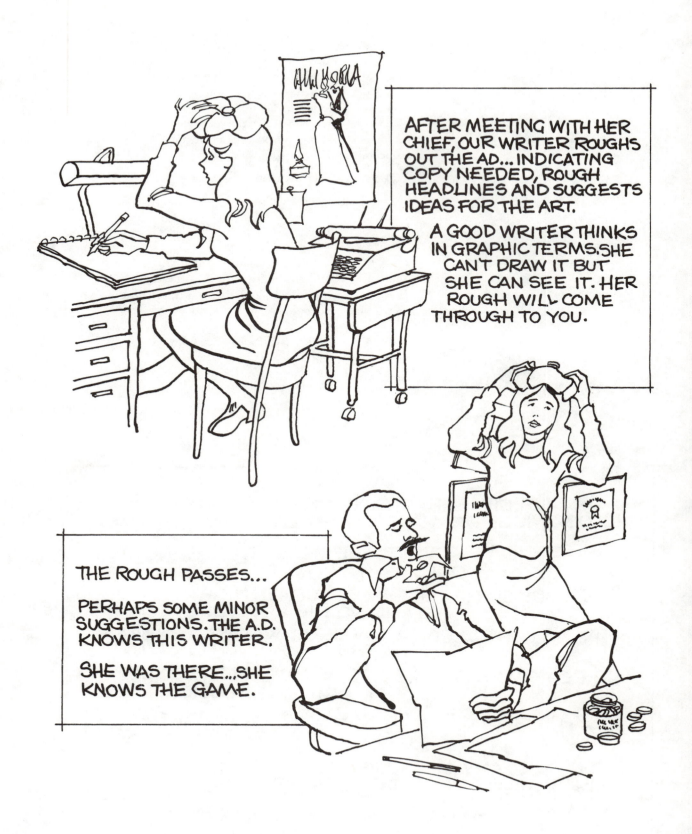

AFTER MEETING WITH HER CHIEF, OUR WRITER ROUGHS OUT THE AD... INDICATING COPY NEEDED, ROUGH HEADLINES AND SUGGESTS IDEAS FOR THE ART.

A GOOD WRITER THINKS IN GRAPHIC TERMS. SHE CAN'T DRAW IT BUT SHE CAN SEE IT. HER ROUGH WILL COME THROUGH TO YOU.

THE ROUGH PASSES...

PERHAPS SOME MINOR SUGGESTIONS. THE A.D. KNOWS THIS WRITER.

SHE WAS THERE...SHE KNOWS THE GAME.

5

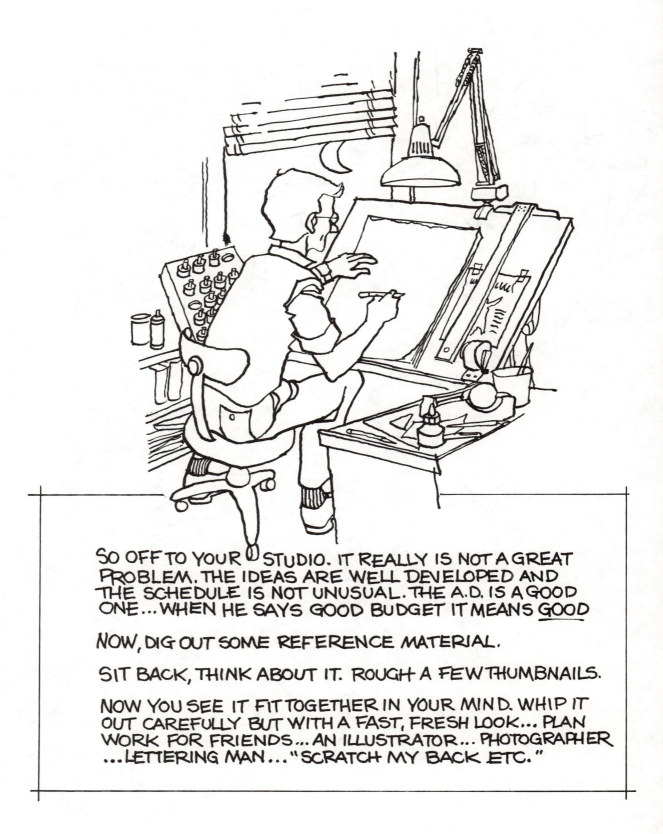

SO OFF TO YOUR STUDIO. IT REALLY IS NOT A GREAT PROBLEM. THE IDEAS ARE WELL DEVELOPED AND THE SCHEDULE IS NOT UNUSUAL. THE A.D. IS A GOOD ONE... WHEN HE SAYS GOOD BUDGET IT MEANS <u>GOOD</u>

NOW, DIG OUT SOME REFERENCE MATERIAL.

SIT BACK, THINK ABOUT IT. ROUGH A FEW THUMBNAILS.

NOW YOU SEE IT FIT TOGETHER IN YOUR MIND. WHIP IT OUT CAREFULLY BUT WITH A FAST, FRESH LOOK... PLAN WORK FOR FRIENDS... AN ILLUSTRATOR... PHOTOGRAPHER ... LETTERING MAN... "SCRATCH MY BACK ETC."

SUCCESS! NOBODY IS REALLY SUPRISED. THE TEAM HAS WORKED TOGETHER ENOUGH SO THAT EVERYBODY KNEW IT WOULD BE RIGHT. THAT IS WHY THEY CALLED <u>YOU</u>!

(IT STILL FEELS GOOD, ANYWAY)

Your layout has met with a gratifying reception which may not seem altogether deserved. It has no particular distinction; it is perhaps a bit old-hat—especially in the present era of the Big Photograph and small copy. Let's analyze it:

It tells the story quickly and succinctly.

It covers all the bases. It immediately attempts to convert a liability into an asset by translating offensive odors into romantic properties. It establishes glamor and macho in the illustration. It shows the product to advantage, even adds a mystic appeal.

It could suggest a packaging approach.

It channels work in the direction of your friends.

AND . . . it is in the client's hands on time.

SO...
WE GO INTO
PRODUCTION

FIRST STOP, THE PRODUCTION MANAGER. HERE THE ROUTING IS ESTABLISHED. 6 COPIES TO THE A.D., 1 EACH TO THE WRITER, THE COPY CHIEF, MAYBE THE BUSINESS OFFICE. 4 TO PRODUCTION DEPARTMENT.

BEFORE DUPLICATING, THE SCHEDULE WILL BE PLANNED AND WRITTEN ON THE LAYOUT FOR ALL CONCERNED TO TRY TO AVOID FOUL-UPS ALONG THE LINE.

(REFER TO MURPHY'S LAW #1)

TYPE SPECIFICATIONS, CHARACTER COUNT (NUMBER OF LETTERS IN THE COPY) WILL ALSO BE WRITTEN ON THE LAYOUT FOR THE WRITER.

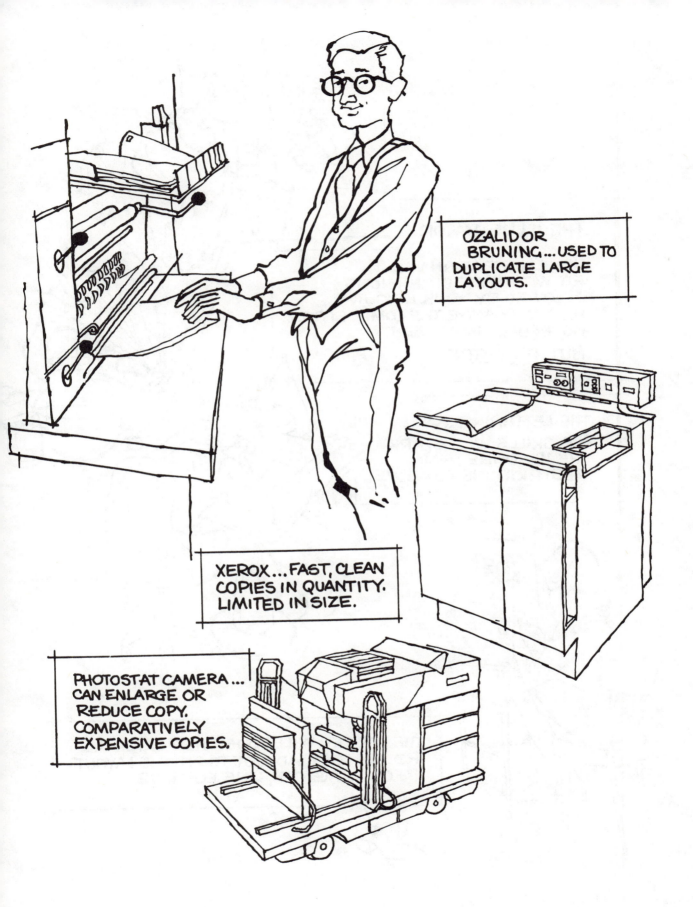

OZALID OR BRUNING...USED TO DUPLICATE LARGE LAYOUTS.

XEROX...FAST, CLEAN COPIES IN QUANTITY. LIMITED IN SIZE.

PHOTOSTAT CAMERA... CAN ENLARGE OR REDUCE COPY. COMPARATIVELY EXPENSIVE COPIES.

THE ILLUSTRATOR

HIS ILLUSTRATION WILL
FIT WITHIN THE DIMENSIONS
ALLOWED BY YOUR LAYOUT.
HE MAY CHANGE THE COMPOSITION,
HOPEFULLY IMPROVE IT
BUT IT MUST FIT!

THE LETTERING MAN...
HIS SKILLS WILL SPARK
THE HEADLINE. SAME
RESTRICTIONS AS ABOVE.

THE WRITER WILL POLISH HER ORIGINAL
ROUGH COPY, ADJUST TO FIT THE LAYOUT
REQUIREMENTS, LINE FOR LINE.

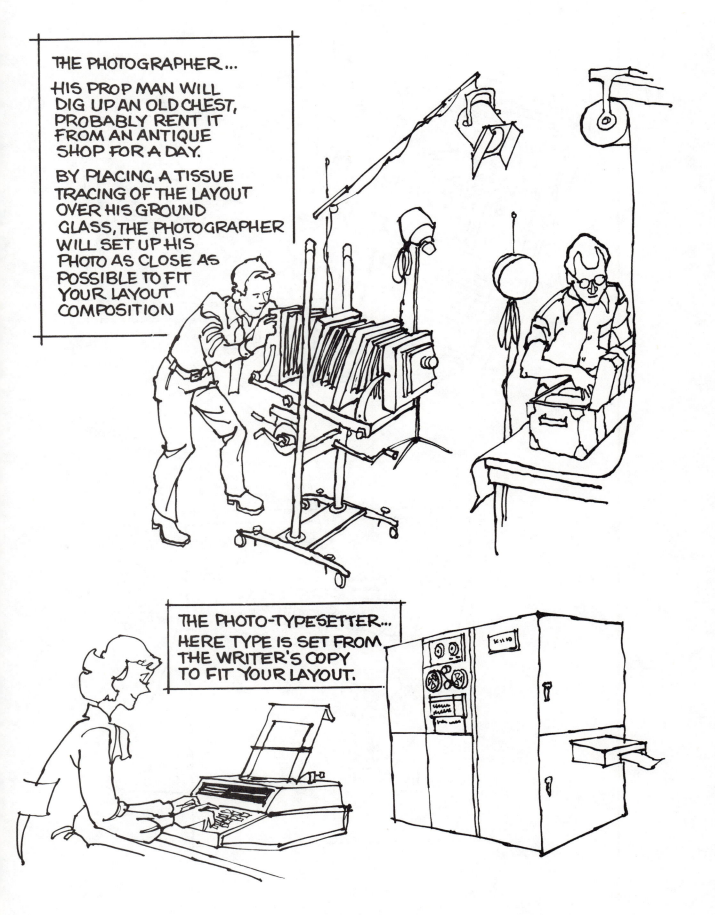

THE PHOTOGRAPHER...

HIS PROP MAN WILL DIG UP AN OLD CHEST, PROBABLY RENT IT FROM AN ANTIQUE SHOP FOR A DAY.

BY PLACING A TISSUE TRACING OF THE LAYOUT OVER HIS GROUND GLASS, THE PHOTOGRAPHER WILL SET UP HIS PHOTO AS CLOSE AS POSSIBLE TO FIT YOUR LAYOUT COMPOSITION

THE PHOTO-TYPESETTER... HERE TYPE IS SET FROM THE WRITER'S COPY TO FIT YOUR LAYOUT.

ALL THE ELEMENTS OF THE AD ULTIMATELY REACH THE BOARD OF THE KEYLINER (PASTE UP MAN, PRODUCTION ARTIST) FOR ASSEMBLY INTO ONE UNIT OF CAMERA-READY COPY (MECHANICAL, ART-BOARD OR KEYLINE). HE WILL PHOTOSTAT ALL OVERSIZE ART (USUALLY 1/2 UP, OR 50% LARGER THAN PRINTING SIZE) OVERPRINTS, STRIP-INS ETC. WILL BE PASTED ON ACETATE OVERLAYS.

THE INSTRUCTIONS OF THIS PRECISE ARTIST WILL CLEARLY DIRECT THE PLATEMAKERS.

THE SUCCESS OF THE EFFORTS OF ALL CONCERNED RESTS WITH THE SKILLS OF THE KEYLINE ARTIST.

16

This brief tour through the active life of a layout demonstrates the importance of your thinking, your imagination, your drawing and compositional skills, *and* your integrity.

Integrity? Attention to typographic and photographic realities. When you drew the old chest, you didn't distort it for effects which the camera could not achieve.

You did not resort to "rubber type." Modern phototypographers can handle almost every kind of distortion, but they cannot (and would not) accommodate this favorite trick of layout cheats.

Rubber type is usually accurate at the ends of a line, faked in the middle; it is a way to present type of a certain size in a width that actually cannot hold it.

If you are provided with manuscript you must learn to "cast copy"; to translate the typewritten lines to lines of type suitable for the body copy or text. It is not difficult.

Pick an average line of the manuscript, without too many caps (capital letters) and count the characters (letters, numerals and spaces between words). For example, the manuscript below has been typed with an average of sixty characters

per line. Then count the number of lines in the manuscript. There are 12 lines in this manuscript, with a total (approximate) of 720 characters. If the lines are very jagged on the right, a vertical pencil line at the average point will help you estimate the additional characters. (Remember, spaces between words count as characters.)

If you have a type specimen book, you may find that it has a line of both pica and elite typewriter type with character count. The same line will then be set in the type sizes suitable for body copy or text. Thus you can measure and determine how many picas or inches are needed to set 40 characters, and then how many picas or inches of copy are needed to set the entire manuscript.

For example, 11-point Bodoni will set 40 characters on a 17-pica (2 13/16") column width. Therefore, about 18 lines will be needed to set the copy 17 picas wide, or half as many lines if you want to set it 34 picas wide. The length of line is your option. It's the total character count that is important.

If you do not have a type book, you should either buy one or see if you can get one from a typographer. Meanwhile, I suggest that you pick a copy block from a magazine and use it as a guide for character count and space needed.

If you are provided with manuscript you must learn to "cast copy"; to translate the typewritten lines to lines of type suitable for the body copy or text. It is not difficult.

Pick an average line of the manuscript, without too many caps (capital letters) and count the characters (letters). For example, this manuscript has been typed with an average of sixty characters per line. Then count the number of lines in the manuscript. There are 12 lines in this manuscript, with a total (approximate) of 720 characters. If the lines are very jagged on the right, a vertical pencil line at the average point will help you estimate the additional characters.

If you have a type specimen book, you may find that it has a line

The cameraman on page 16 will be shooting a "combination highlight halftone." To explain this title in reverse: the art (meaning entire art-board) is photographed with a halftone screen between the lens and the film. This screen, with perhaps 250 lines both horizontal and vertical to a square inch, breaks up the art into dots. The more light reflected from the art, the bigger the dot. Thus on the *negative,* the white areas will have the largest dots. Inversely, on the printing plate (which, like a photographic print, is the positive image), they will be the smallest and print the least.

A "highlight" halftone is one in which these white areas have been opaqued on the negative by hand so that no dots at all will appear on the plate.

The "combination" part means that the art will also be shot in line (without the screen) and the two negatives combined to make the plate so that solid blacks will print solid, without tiny dots that would grey them.

LET'S
BANISH
THE
GRID...OR,
I FOR ONE
MISS THE

To be serious about your profession, you must become a serious student of contemporary design, both in the galleries and on the printed page—both "fine art" and "commercial."

What is happening now in the best galleries will probably soon show up on the printed page. Part of the problem with today's advertising design is the recent lack of any strong trend or directional influence from the galleries.

Two major influences have dominated the printed page for many years: The Grid System and the Push-Pin Studios Approach. The oldest and easiest to utilize (or imitate) is the *Bauhaus–Swiss grid system.* For this the artist draws a geometric grid based either on classic rules of symmetry or on proportions of his or her own invention. Using this grid as a guide, he designs his layouts to fit the set proportions. At their best, layouts created on a grid are spare, crisp, and highly communicative. At their worst, man-handled by a poor imitator, they are deadly dull. The two layouts above (each stolen from a national magazine ad) are grid layouts. I do not accuse them of being deadly dull, but they don't excite me. They're "very nice" but not "hey, wow!"

During the past twenty years or so, an entirely different look created by one studio, Push-Pin Studios, shook up the industry. At Push-Pin, some of the country's best designers launched a new, personal style that was sometimes nostalgic, sometimes revolutionary, and always offbeat.

At their best, layouts imitating the Push-Pin style are exciting, innovative, and quick to communicate. At their worst, they are schlock (politely translated as "junk"). The four layouts on the opposite page look back nostalgically for their inspiration. Buck Rogers of the thirties, sheet music of the twenties, nineteenth-century posters, and John Held, Jr. of the thirties. Unfortunately, they do not interpret those styles—they copy. They try to use the past creatively, but unlike Push-Pin designs, they are derivative.

They can be classified under another enjoyable name, *kitsch*—not directly translatable but referring to "cheap finery," or bad taste. Kitsch these layouts are . . . but fun, exciting, and communicative. Highly derivative in design, but strong and individual in character.

21

Before the serious onslaught of the BIG Photo, there were many derivative, but fun, trends. The layout above is like many of the imitations of Peter Max. Peter Max came forth with a uniquely decorative powdered-sugar confection that was all his own. New. Expressive of his time. Prosperity. Top-of-the-world America.

And just about everybody latched on. The printed page jumped with pink clouds, blue flowers, and funny dancing people. Peter Max made a million, and millions had to live through it.

Out of Haight-Ashbury came the psychedelic poster with its loud, countercultural, and often soft-porn graphics. Another bandwagon had arrived and it was fun to jump on and enjoy it without being subjected to the fervor and the acid (pun) emotionalism of the originators. Kitsch again, but it was exciting to work on one of those layouts.

Still with us is the influence of Art Nouveau. Not an overnight movement, the Art Nouveau school has provided a wealth of decorative, imaginative styles and symbols that are easily converted to layout design. Unlike those who imitate Peter Max or the psychedelic posters, people who want to utilize the abundant symbols of Art Nouveau can legitimately design in an established tradition—they don't copy an entity.

Like Art Nouveau, Art Deco has sufficient vitality to return repeatedly to print. It is more difficult to translate because of the restrictive nature of its symbols. Because of its built-in excitement, it persists. Art Deco has been reactivated lately because of a new interest among collectors, several new books, and because it offers some refuge from the BIG Photograph.

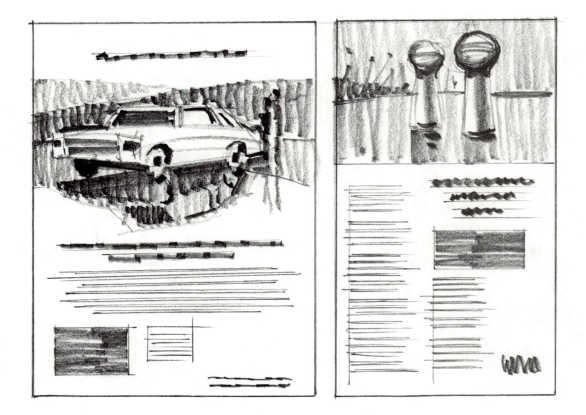

"So," you say to yourself, "where do I go from here?" Let's go along looking and thinking for just a bit. Opposite page top left shows an ad that appeared nationally. The BIG Photograph still (of a car, reflected in water), but all in all, a pretty good layout. Nice play of blacks, pleasing distribution of white space (also called "air").

Not long after this campaign was launched, three imitators appeared in the *New York Times* on the same Sunday. All were cosmetic ads placed by department stores. These are almost always large ads because cosmetic manufacturers cooperate in paying for the ads which are charged to the stores at "local" rates which are much lower than rates charged to "national" advertisers.

Heck, you could latch on to that theme and do a beautiful job. Like the two above. Not a thing wrong with them, but they sure are derivative!

And you would like to be creative and at least somewhat original.

Consider the following two pages of thumbnail layouts made from the first eight pages of ads in recent *Time, Vogue, McCall's,* and *Fortune* magazines. These ads comprise only a small part of a great arid desert of monotonous design that currently fills most of our print media. The BIG Photograph. Advertisers dependent totally on the quality of a photograph. Layout artists, perhaps not by choice, ignoring the opportunities for exciting visual communication. I have marked the merchandise or objective of each of these ads. The layouts would never convey it.

VOGUE

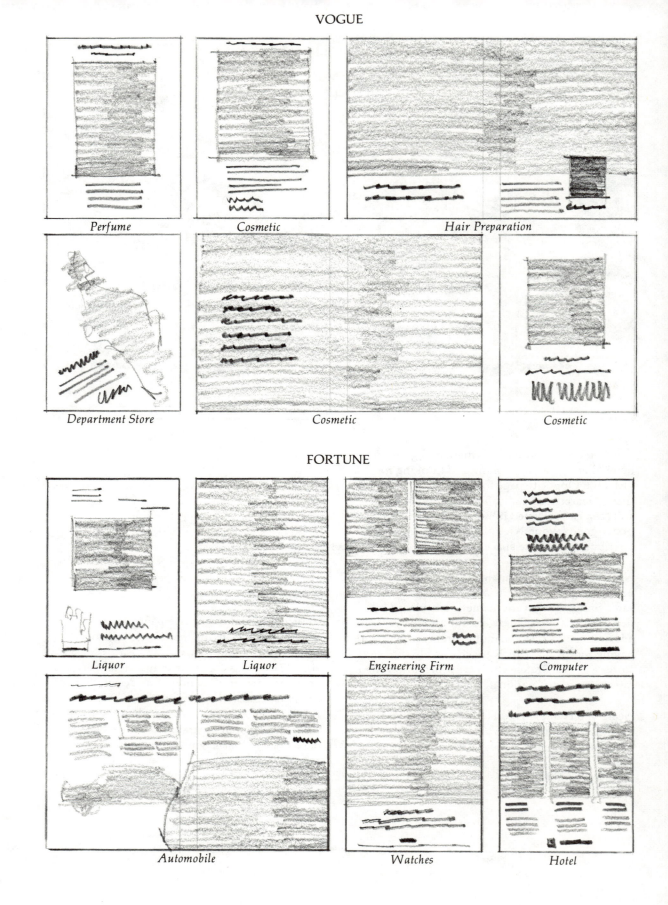

Perfume

Cosmetic

Hair Preparation

Department Store

Cosmetic

Cosmetic

FORTUNE

Liquor

Liquor

Engineering Firm

Computer

Automobile

Watches

Hotel

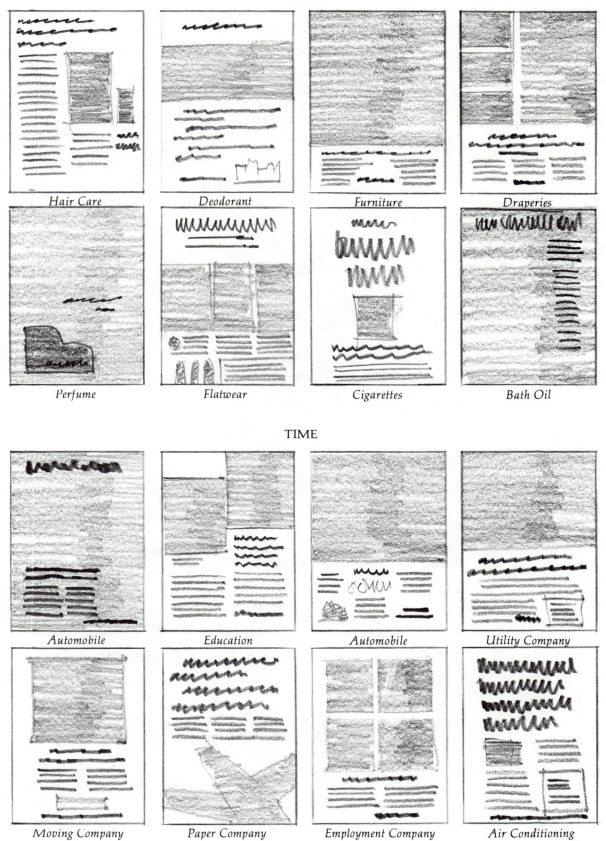

Hair Care

Deodorant

Furniture

Draperies

Perfume

Flatwear

Cigarettes

Bath Oil

TIME

Automobile

Education

Automobile

Utility Company

Moving Company

Paper Company

Employment Company

Air Conditioning

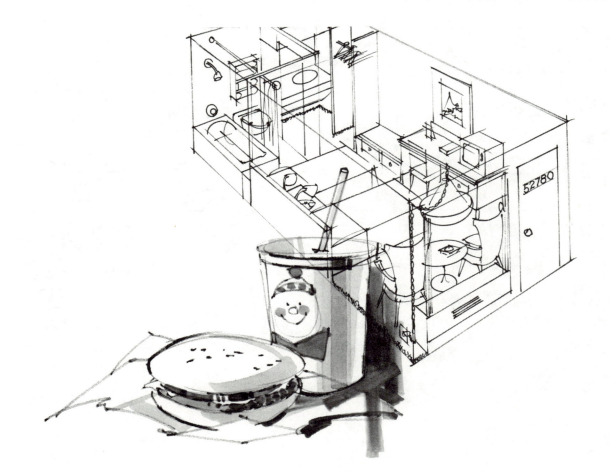

SUMMING UP

Layouts based on a grid—up-to-the-minute looking. Clean, crisp, serene designs with a peaceful, unprovocative balance.

Layouts imitating the creative approaches of Push-Pin Studios: fun, exciting, Kitschy . . . derivative

Layouts which join the crowd in new trends: fun for a short while, quickly boring.

Layouts dependent on the BIG Photograph— monotony.

Can you sit down and draw every motel room you can remember? Was the only question that of whether there would be a separation for the lavatory or just for the toilet and tub?

Is your only question about the next hamburger whether it will have caraway seeds?

SNORE . . .

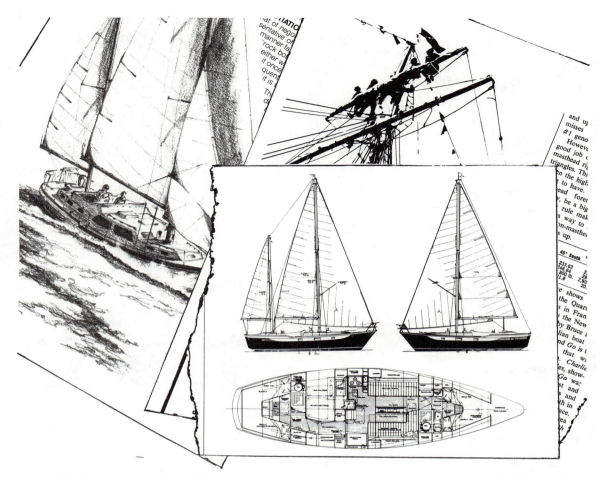

O.K. Mr. Smart—where do we start?

I start with the assumption that this King Cay man with his polished brass and mahogany, etc., is a seafarer. Whether modern or costume doesn't matter. So I dig out some swipes (clippings of art from magazines, newspapers, etc.) as a starter. If necessary, I buy a copy of *Yachting* and tear out some pages that communicate to me. Not their message—just the shapes, striking some sort of spark in the back of my mind.

I slide a swipe under the layout sheet, move it around to see if I can visualize it working with type, and then lay in bold, broad tones with a pencil. My brain seems to respond only when my hand pushes a pencil.

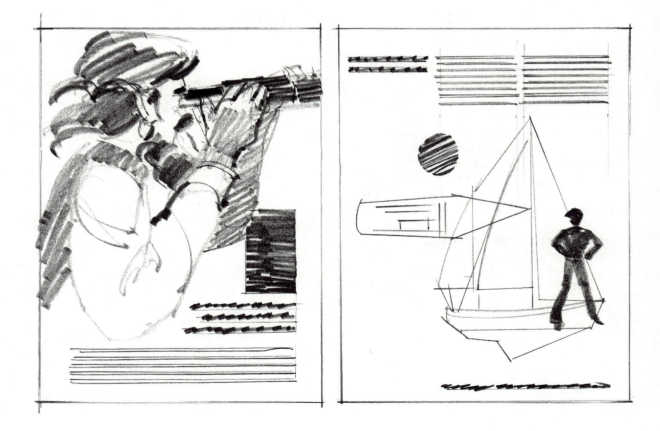

Here are the first five roughs that came along after the pencil started working. Three of them departed completely from the swipes; one of them (lower right) turned into a grid-type layout without the grid.

One (upper left, opposite) may be too copy-heavy and one that I like (upper right, opposite) may stray too far from the requirements: the man, the product. However, I would have no qualms about discussing any of them with the art director.

Try it. Let your pencil lead you along and see what happens. Will you surprise and maybe astound yourself? That is the big question. What you are after in a small rough like this is the color (sure there is color in black and white!), the values, contrasts, and balances—not the content of the drawing. In order to get the most from your pencil you need a good drawing grip. See page 100 for one suggested grip.

Stroke in your values. Don't shade, and above all, don't outline. The 2B pencil is happiest on a bond or vellum paper. On flimsy tracing paper, newsprint, or that weird stuff used in a lot of drawing classes, the pencil is weak and unhappy. A 2B pencil can do *anything* if it is kept crisp— crisp meaning that even when not pointed sharp, it maintains sharp, clean edges on the flat side. (Your drawing grip should be using the side of the lead.) When the edges of your strokes start getting fuzzy, sharpen the pencil again.

Use directional strokes freely. Notice the way broad strokes, horizontal, vertical, and diagonal are boldly used in these roughs . . . and how well they work in contrast to the loose, light descriptive lines of the sleeve, the faces.

Don't fuss with your drawing, and avoid erasures. Better to use the drawing as an underlay than to do a lot of erasing. Keep it spontaneous; use the eraser only to clean up white space.

There is no "right" way to design a layout other than by planning and by using your imagination. There are pitfalls (and pratfalls) scattered around the path that should be avoided, and the most blatant is schlock. As defined earlier, this is trashy thinking and comes in many forms.

Here are half a dozen.

Starting from the lower left, with an example of an ad that was almost good but succumbed to too many overprints and reverses, too much activity. Could be called good schlock. Then there is the typical drugstore schlock above with its screaming reverses, crowded design, tasteless hodgepodge of elements. Next to it is a typographic nightmare that manages to use three different scripts and two sizes of display type jumbled together with four separate pieces of art.

For Your File:

SIMPLICITY SIMPLICITY SIMPLICITY

Build large elements in your design. Hear warning bells when you reach for more than two sizes of display type.

These three ads represent a different kind of schlocky thinking. While the layouts are strong and do not suffer from the physical ailments of those opposite, these are all victims of cheap thinking . . . kitsch, again.

Top left is a cutesy thought that probably flipped out both its creator and his client. It is just about as good as a plastic Venus de Milo on your mantel. Next to it soft-porn schlock. The designer who has to reach to porn to convey the message cannot have much of a graphic vocabulary.

And below, the layout artist has jumped on another bandwagon of current chic but has fallen right off again by letting the kitschy gimmick overpower the art, the message, and the reader.

All of these layouts are pratfalls. Don't expose yourself to the embarrassment of admitting you created junk like this.

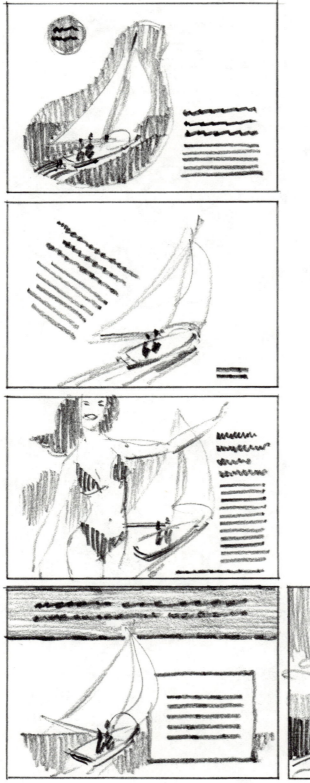

Tired Clichés . . .

Artificial shapes. Don't impose forms on your message. The natural shape of the elements is much more interesting.

Tilted typography. Consider the hazards of reading tipped type on a crowded bus. Don't complicate life for your reader.

The extraneous feature. Don't hide your message behind a gimmick. You are trying to communicate—your reader is not going to hunt for your message.

Boxes. Don't break up your space—unify it. The idea is to make it bigger, stronger.

Mortices. Like boxes, mortices break up space. Find a better way to design the copy area.

SIMPLICITY SIMPLICITY SIMPLICITY

COMPLICATIONS . . .

Conflicting elements. Don't destroy one symbol in a head-on collision with another: especially with all that room to maneuver.

Dangerous overprints. There is no type in text sizes that could possibly be read over sky, clouds, and deep sea.

Chasing contours. If you already have the art, it can be done, but the result is hardly worth the loving care needed.

Unnatural vignettes. A workable vignette needs reasonable forms (trees, arms, legs, something to establish an edge)—water and sky fade into uninteresting mush.

Widely split headlines. Don't break a line of display type to this extent. Use discretion—give the reader a break.

SIMPLICITY SIMPLICITY SIMPLICITY

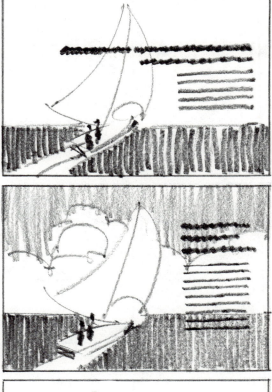

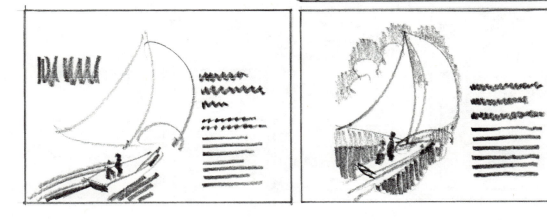

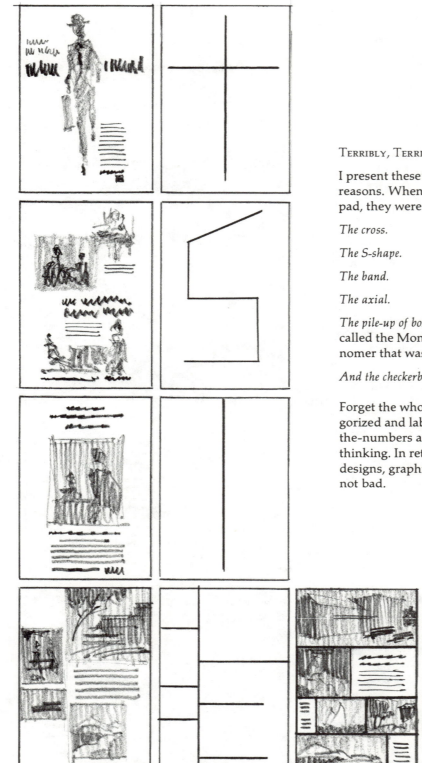

Terribly, Terribly Tired Clichés . . .

I present these poor little fellows for sentimental reasons. When I was first exposed to a layout pad, they were teaching this kind of nonsense.

The cross.

The S-shape.

The band.

The axial.

The pile-up of boxes. This one was affectionately called the Mondrian. What a miserable misnomer that was!

And the checkerboard (opposite lower right).

Forget the whole bunch. Design cannot be categorized and labeled. Layouts are not paint-by-the-numbers affairs. They demand hard work, thinking. In return—the joy of turning out solid designs, graphics that communicate. And that is not bad.

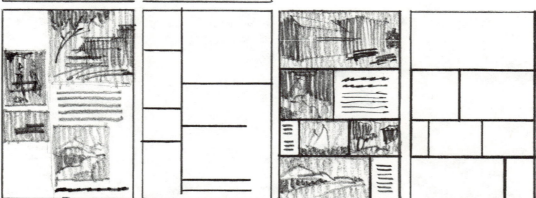

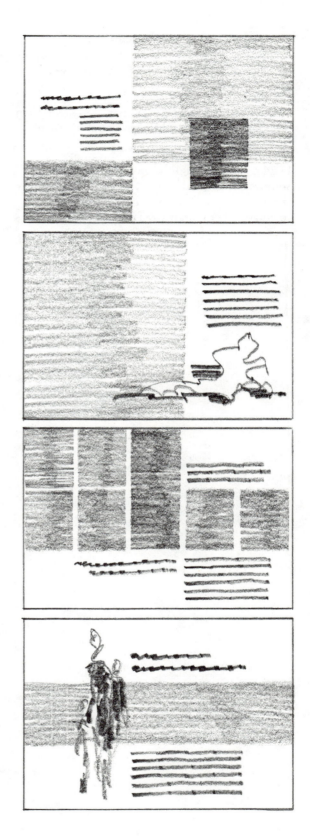

And finally, back where we started this chapter . . . a very simplified grid and layouts done from it. There is absolutely no question that the geometrics of these layouts are pleasing. The family resemblance (the continuity of design which ties a series of layouts together) is strong and the balances are excellent.

Acceptable results come quickly and easily. So what is the big objection?

They could have been done by a computer.

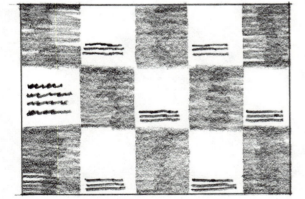

What counts is what is spontaneous, impulsive. That is the truthful truth. What we impose upon ourselves does not emanate from ourselves.

—*Picasso*

I would rather invent a grammar of my own than bind myself to rules which don't belong to me.

—*Picasso*

I still reserve the right at any time to doubt the solutions furnished by the Modulor, keeping intact my freedom, which must depend on my feelings rather than my reason.

—*Le Corbusier*

70% of all commissions in graphic design must satisfy the communication needs of industry and advertising.

[the artist] must accept the contrast between self-realization and practice.

The idea, however, is inimitable—the idea is and remains an individual phenomenon.

—*Professor Albrecht Ade*
GHS Wuppertal, Grafik-Design

GETTING STARTED

Here are the basic tools necessary to put your images on paper: from left to right at random.

Layout pad. Invest in a best-quality vellum pad. 19″ × 24″. It will be expensive. Save the scraps for extra mileage.

T-square. 24″ is best. (Check for squareness—many are off.)

Triangles. Any triangle with 10″ to 12″ hypotenuse is fine.

Fixative. The workable kind is advised. Workable meaning that the fixed surface can be penetrated for further rendering.

18″ ruler. Get one with pica and agate lines.

Kneaded eraser. Best. Can be shaped for delicate

areas, cleans well.

Masking tape and scotch tape.

Pencils. 2B recommended. Chisel edge if you have had training in its use.

X-acto knife or razor blade.

Typing paper.

There are three basic type styles:

Serif faces. These have small lines (serifs) at top and bottom of verticals and diagonals and usually vary in the width of strokes. Serif styles are classified as Old Style, with curves flowing into the serifs, and Modern, with light, flat serifs.

Square serif faces.

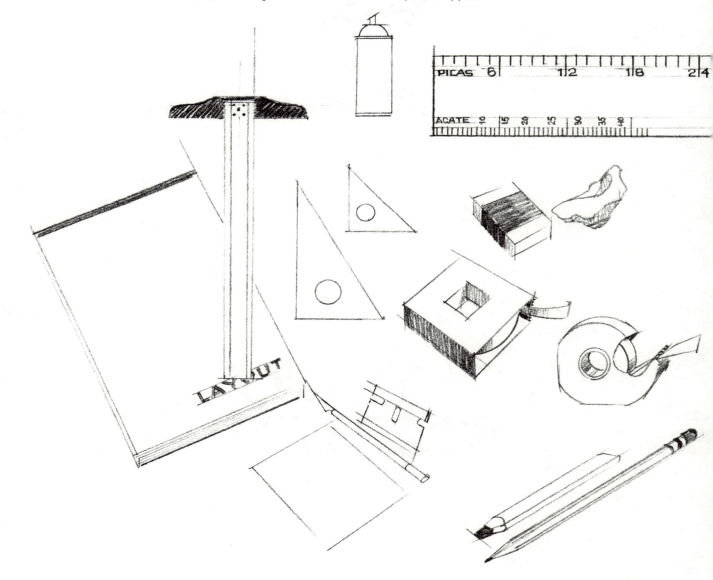

Most of these are designed with equal strokes.

Sans serif faces.   These are without serifs (French: *sans*, without). Many varieties available, old to ultra-modern.

Most fonts (all the letters available in one face, one size) are designed in both Roman, upright, and Italic, slanting. Many have "extended" and "condensed" as well as bold and extra-bold versions. Large type used in headlines is termed "display," while the small type is called "body copy" or "text."

Text is indicated on a layout by a double line that represents the "x-height" or body of the lower-case (small) letters (a, c, e, o, etc.) without risers (b, d, f, h, k, l) or descenders (g, j, p, q).

The space between the double line indications is usually deeper to accommodate risers and descenders with a little air added for legibility. The airing of text is called "leading," and is a carry-over term from the days of metal type (hot type) when strips of lead as thin as 1 point were used to separate lines of type. Today, most type is set on film (cold type) and spacing of lines is just another part of the computerized process.

The three copy blocks at the bottom of this page show copy set "flush left and right," "fl L stagger R," and "fl R stagger L." Dark lines show different ways to indicate bold-face lead-ins.

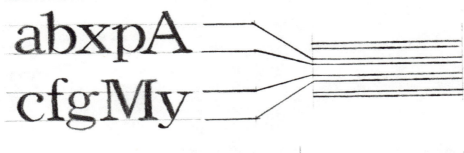

Old Style *italics*

Modern **bold**

Square condensed

Sans serif extended

abxpA
cfgMy

I can suggest several ways to get over the initial fear of the blank layout pad:

1. Tear the cover off. This will show your confidence and lessen your awe of such an expensive pad of paper.

2. Take your T-square in hand and draw the dimensions of your ad. Getting some lines on the paper always helps. Always in pencil. A felt-tip marker or pen line is too permanent, too restrictive. Keep your options open.

3. Do some thumbnails to get the feel of the pencil and paper.

4. Slide a swipe, any swipe, under the layout sheet to diminish the blankness.

Hey, I rather like that thumbnail on the left. How do we develop it? First, a type that will create an action similar to the strong black at the top. Here's a square serif face that seems to have the right feel. Rockwell Antique, 42 pt.

Put the type sheet under your layout paper, down near the bottom where you can cut it off. Draw guidelines top and bottom of the caps.

Now roughly trace the letters so that the weight is expressed. Do not outline or trace lightly. You can't get the feel of the letters, nor can you space them well, without a true indication of the weight.

Next, eyeball (estimate roughly) the area you think the drawing can occupy and make a loose, rough drawing on a piece of your typing paper.

You now have a good start on the two most important elements in your layout.

NEVER FORGET! LAYOUT DRAWING IS NOT ILLUSTRATION.

Slide the type indication and drawing under the space indication. On my layout, the type is obviously too big and the mermaid's tail won't fit. A matter of minutes to rough the letters in 36 pt. and draw a new tail. Back under the layout area, tip the art to a steeper angle, split the type to two lines . . . there it is.

Next, I render the art; hitting the contrasts hardest around his head, eliminating the excess drawing, trying to build a diagonal tonal area to repeat the action of the boom. Then I push the rough type around to find the best spot, draw guidelines, and *use the type sheet* again; more carefully tracing the letters.

Then line in the copy. We have liberty in speci-

fying the amount of copy because it is unwritten. Finally, position the photo of the bottle for best use of the black accent, and line in the bold copy.

The most important lesson so far is to *maintain your mobility.* By the use of underlays, keep the widest choice of options open as long as possible. Repeat, never draw the outline of a space in ink or pentel. You may want to adjust the space surrounding the elements of a finished, or nearly finished layout. Space indications in pencil can be erased, the space can move.

The space, except for its dimensions, is unimportant. The elements in the space actually create it. Otherwise it is a big blank, a void. Your thinking makes it . . . or breaks it.

POTPOURRI...

For Your File:

Here is a random collection of good ways to do little things that will help your work.

For a crisp, straight edge of a tone, broad-stroke your pencil against the triangle. Let the little whites remain. Don't draw the shape and try to fill in.

The reverse—for a crisp, white edge cutting out of a tone area, wipe across a sheet of typing paper into the tone with the kneaded eraser. If the top or bottom of a line of type looks too jagged, use the same technique.

Have to divide an odd length equally or in related percentages? Draw a vertical at one end of the length. Hold your ruler at the other end and tip it up the vertical until you come to a divisible dimension. Then drop verticals back to the original length and you have it.

Need to scale a space? Smaller for a thumbnail, for example? Draw a diagonal. All spaces, no matter how big, that incorporate that same diagonal, will be in scale with each other.

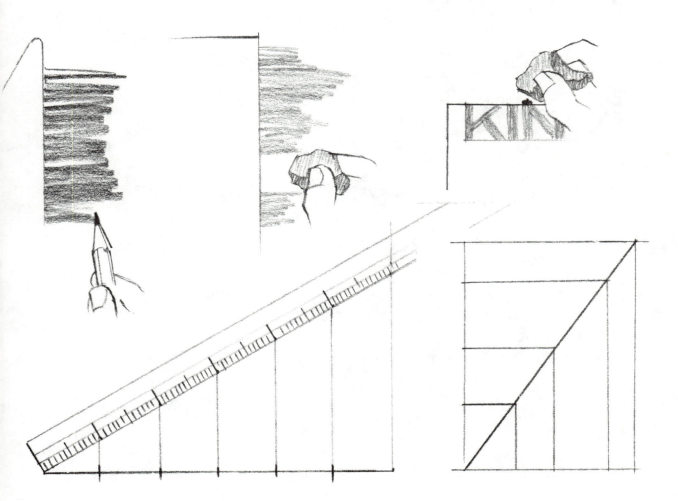

Patching.   A very important minor skill. Don't try to paint or scratch an unerasable error. Patch it for best results.

To patch, tape a scrap of layout paper over the area of error, re-render it correctly on the scrap. Stick a piece of cardboard under the layout sheet (you don't want to cut right through the pad) and with a razor blade or X-acto knife, cut through both pieces of paper at once. Tape the new patch into the layout from the back with scotch tape. Properly done, it will be almost invisible.

For larger patches, where the whole type area just didn't work out, or someone spilled ink or beer (don't laugh), it is best to cut the patch along a drawing edge, as indicated below, right. This way, the only part of the patch that will ever show will be from the leg to the edge of the layout.

Think about it, though. Sometimes it is *much* faster to re-render than do all the cutting and taping. Hard to accept, but very true. You will (as I did) undoubtedly learn it the hard way.

Space Descriptions, Magazines

You are running a third of a page in a magazine with a three-column format. One column is 110 agate lines. The column width is two inches. The magazine offers a one-third page ad in two shapes: one column full (2″ by 110 agate lines) or on two columns (4″ by 55 agate lines). The small rough shows you your choices. The magazine will *not* run two one-column ads next to each other, but it might run two with a column of editorial between. It *will* run two two-column by 55 agate line spaces together. Your design must protect your space.

For the Trivia File:

Tapes, scotch and masking, lift off vellum with ease. Tend to tear the surface of bond. Don't tape on or near a drawing on bond.

Clean T-square and triangle regularly with a kneaded eraser. They accumulate pencil dust and can dirty a layout.

To fix a pencil layout, spray lightly from about a foot. After drying, give it a heavier coat. Pencil bleeds badly if sprayed heavily at first.

Repeat.   Minimize erasures, especially on bond. Leave the errors. Many turn out to be of no consequence or even assets.

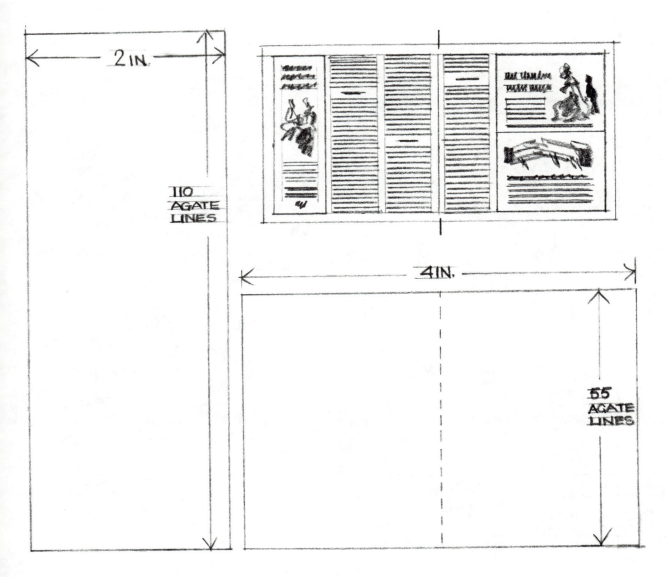

On *bleed pages* art goes right out to the edge. Magazines specify the bleed size, the trim (final size of page), and the "live matter" area within which all type and important art should be kept.

Catalog layouts call for minimum rendering. Writers usually provide clips from earlier catalogs for copy "specs" (specifications). The artist draws a rectangle with two diagonals. The art is outlined in pencil with a flat overall tone. "Co-op" pages (where manufacturer pays part or all) may call for more comp rendering, especially in color.

Magazine editorial layouts are usually thumbnails with instructions written on the side. Will vary from doodles to concise miniature layouts.

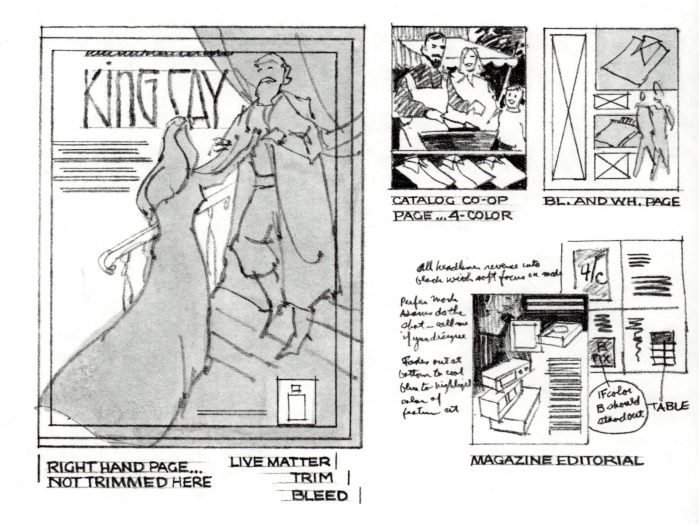

RIGHT HAND PAGE...
NOT TRIMMED HERE

LIVE MATTER
TRIM
BLEED

CATALOG CO-OP
PAGE ...4-COLOR

BL. AND WH. PAGE

MAGAZINE EDITORIAL

Newspapers usually specify space in inches, though some use agate lines. An eight-column page, 21″ deep, would be specified as 168″ (8 col. × 21″). Most newspapers are eight-column. (The *New York Times* has recently switched to six columns in many of its sections, but it is an exception.) Tabloid newspapers are usually 6-columns. A half-page, or 84″ space can be run in several shapes. Divide the space, 84″, by the number of columns for the shapes shown below. Similarly, spaces of one through seven columns can vary in shape. A common limitation is that the depth in inches must exceed the width in columns. Oddly, many newspapers accept long, flat ads (eight-column by 2 or 3 inches) on the sports page only.

Retail advertisers often use a step-down ad that is really two spaces used as one. *Example:* a five-column by 10″ space with a three-column by 14″ space next to it for a total space of 92 column inches.

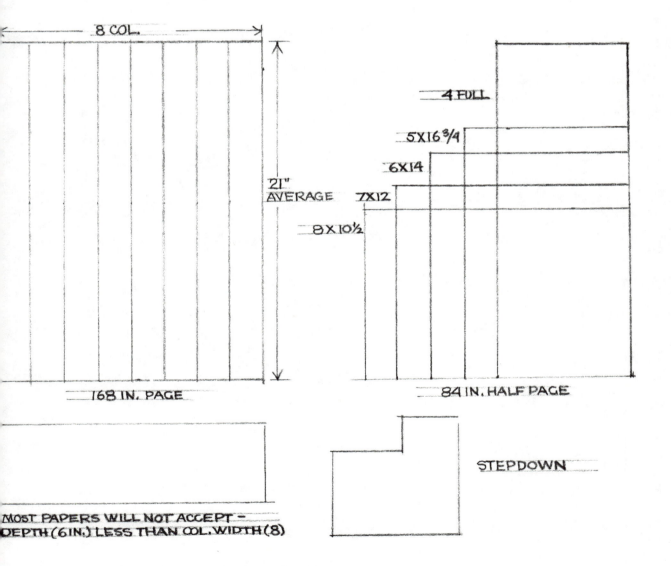

Discarding a layout that started well but went sour is one of the hardest things we face. We re-work, patch, and erase . . . and all the time we know deep down inside . . . it's no good.

It happens to everyone.

There is little advice to be given. The best thing to do is to use it as an underlay and get a fresh start. Usually, the second try will progress at an astonishing pace because in your mind the troubles have been solved. All the necessary elements are in the failure . . . just in the wrong places.

Don't cherish the sick layout. Make it work for you and then throw it away.

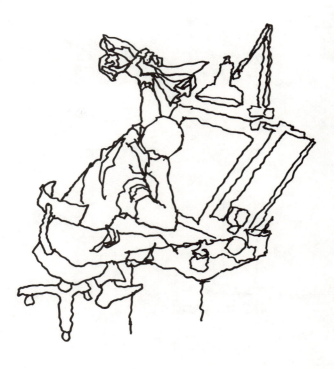

Although not absolutely necessary, a knowledge of proofreaders' marks is a definite asset to the layout artist. On the left in caps are those that are most important to the artist, followed by a listing (in lowercase) of commonly used marks.

e	DELETE
#	INSERT SPACE
⌣	LESS SPACE
◯	CLOSE UP; DELETE SPACE
tr	TRANSPOSE WORDS THE
bf	SET BOLDFACE
stet	LET IT STAND
¶	START NEW PARAGRAPH
no ¶	NO PARAGRAPH
⊓	RAISE; MOVE UP
⊔	LOWER; MOVE DOWN
[	MOVE LEFT
]	MOVE RIGHT
∧	Left out, insert
9	Inverted letter (type upside down)
X	Broken letter
e/	Correct letter
eq #	Equal space between words
tr	1 3 2 4 5 Rearrange of order words in
lc	Lowercase letter
sm caps	Small capitals
caps and sm. caps	Caps and small caps
≡	Set in caps
C	Cap letter
ital	Set italic
rom	Set roman
bf	Set boldface
lf	Set lightface
‖	Align copy
‖	No indentation
⊙ ∧	Insert period, insert comma
:/ ;/	Insert colon, semicolon
∨ ∨∨	Insert apostrophe, quotation marks
[/] c/)	Insert brackets, parentheses
▫ ▭ ▭	Indent one, two, or three em
out, see copy	Insert matter, omitted
Spell out	Spell out
⸗	Type out of alignment
∨ /3	Superior and inferior letters, numbers

52

pastels, pencils, miscellaneous mediums...

Pastels, which went out of favor when the felt-tip markers changed the whole layout scene, have recently experienced a minor resurgence due to the rapidly rising cost of markers. An excellent rendering medium, pastels are difficult to use and still keep a clean layout. Dust that is invisible before being sprayed with fixative, has a nasty way of popping out when it is too late to erase. Pencils, charcoal, etc., are also good in their place but restricted when rendering large areas. All are worth experiencing.

#2B Pencil

In the previous chapters we have experimented with the extremely potent 2B pencil. Handled correctly, it is an ideal drawing tool. Directional strokes used for volume and values, strong blacks against whites and fine loose lines for definition and contrast.

This drawing has been rubbed with a tissue to achieve soft, feminine tones. Vellum works best for this effect.

Charcoal Pencil

A very good drawing tool, especially useful in conjunction with pastels. Bolder renderings are more possible than with the 2B because the charcoal is blacker than the lead. Rubs well on any paper. Harder to keep the drawing clean.

Pastels

A truly great layout medium. It is most important to keep the paper clean as the drawing progresses and to avoid erasures.

I am using the word "pastels" in the generic sense, referring to any dry stick chalk, rectangular in shape with hard, sharp edges. These black-and-white drawings are actually done with a compressed charcoal stick. Working in color, square stick pastels would be used. I have never found oil-based pastels satisfactory as a layout medium.

Prismacolor Pencils

Not recommended. This pencil, currently much used in illustration, is more adapted to that field. Its hard point and delicate line tends to tighten the drawing and will lead the artist away from layout indication into illustration.

Pastel pencils have much the same characteristics, though they are softer and can be rubbed and smeared for broad effects. Both are useful in conjunction with other mediums, but not as the sole medium for an entire layout.

Watercolor or Wash

While water-based washes have the decided advantage of being applied with a brush and therefore permitting great variety of line and tone, the disadvantages outweigh the benefits. Layout paper will not stand up to much water. This drawing has not affected the paper to any appreciable degree because the large areas were applied with a tissue and very little water actually inpregnated the paper. The brush lines are small enough so that they will not crinkle the paper.

Drawing Ink

Like watercolor, will crinkle paper if used in large areas with a brush. The large areas of black in this drawing have been applied with a brush and immediately wiped with a tissue. In this way the water was prevented from penetrating the paper. The area of tone on the side of the face and in small shadows is not wash. It is a #4 cool grey marker applied on the back of the paper. This is another advantage of a good, heavy vellum.

Acrylics

Striking effects can be achieved through the use of acrylic black with markers. On this drawing, all the large black areas are acrylic applied with a tissue directly from the tube without water. Acrylic used this way dries very quickly. The large tone area is again a #4 on the back and the detail drawing is #4 on the front with black details drawn with a felt-tip pen. Acrylic greys would have to be mixed. Not at all practical.

Retouch Greys

This drawing is rendered with retouch greys and markers. These greys come in a variety of tones similar to the cool grey markers, so there is no mixing problem. The consistency of the paint without water, however, is sticky and not practical for layout drawing. Like the other techniques shown on these two pages, it is a good trick to know for special effects but not for normal rendering.

All the renderings on these two pages were drawn on vellum with a compressed charcoal stick as shown. The important *must* is to maintain sharp edges on the stick. The right end of this stick is in good working order but there will be no more crisp tones or lines from the left end. It should be broken off and thrown away.

The large washy areas were brushed out with a tissue and then lightened and modeled with a kneaded eraser. The sharp blacks were drawn with the edge of the stick and the broad greys drawn with the end, which accounts for the wear that destroyed the left end. White lettering done with white charcoal pencil.

All of these drawings were rendered in the same manner. Broad areas were wiped in with a vigorous, loose stroke with blacks worked in and whites erased out.

The drawing of the glass has been cropped. In a layout, this would be patched in rather than drawn on the layout sheet: this is cleaner than trying to erase for crisp edges.

This drawing on vellum has been heightened by the use of grey markers in the foreground and in the horizontal tones in the sky. Markers work well with stick chalks *after* the drawing has been well fixed (sprayed with fixative).

For Your File:

The quickest way to draw water is to stroke in the broad darks and lights first *vertically* and then go back with surface detail (at a minimum) horizontally.

This drawing on vellum might well be cropped at the sides only. The loose blended tones contrast well with the geometrics of the type. The reverse lettering was done with a brush and white ink after trying it with a charcoal white pencil. The whites did not seem strong enough for reproduction, and ink was used.

MASSACHUSETTS

We have a special place for you!

Your choice of paper when approaching a pastel rendering is important. My preference is consistently for the heavy vellum. To me, it has proven the most versatile, toughest paper and still very transparent.

The drawing on this page has been rendered on a layout bond. With this paper it is largely a matter of putting a stroke down and leaving it alone. It does not rub well (check the lower right corner and right-hand portion of the sky), nor does it erase well.

There is nothing wrong with a drawing that is done simply and directly. A good drawing can be done any way the artist wishes. However, I like to know that my paper will take any techniques I choose.

The drawing opposite was rendered on a very lightweight coated tracing paper. The surface is slick and the chalks ride on it with almost no penetration of the fibers. Consequently, it rubs easily, the effects are soft and misty. Erasing is easy.

Two devices used in this drawing are also shown opposite. On the left I have rubbed a lot of chalk onto a piece of typing paper. Then, by rubbing it off the paper onto the layout, I obtained a soft tone with sharp, clean edge. On the right, I erased into the grey, using the typing paper for a crisp edge.

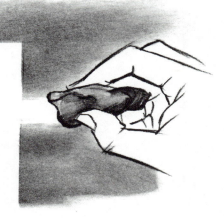

Many years ago, in my first job as an art director, I worked for a very kind but fiery-tempered ad manager. One day he worked up a rage and stood nose to nose with me, calling me every name in the book. Just at the point where my own Irish was reaching the boiling point, he stopped and asked me for a cigarette. At that point, he recognized my bewilderment.

"You aren't taking this personally, are you? I'm not talking about *you*." He poked me in the chest for emphasis. "I'm talking business!" We lit cigarettes and the tirade continued.

Learn as early as possible to be impersonal about criticism. Your layouts are not your children. Defend them (to a degree) if you are right, but never become personally involved. You could probably come up with a new, and maybe better, layout in the time it takes to fight about it.

MARKERS

Different from any drawing tool that most of us have ever used, the broad-tip marker can scare the life out of us. There's only one solution. Pick up a handful and go to work. Literally, hold six or seven in your left hand (if you are right-handed) for easy access. This is simpler than reaching to a box each time you want a different one. Then see what they do . . . all you can lose is a little time and a piece of paper.

Don't try to shade or model as you might with a pencil. Markers are not made for that kind of drawing. They are designed for indication and that is what layout drawing is all about. The left hand above has been doodled quite a bit because I wanted to bring it forward and also stress the handful effect. The right hand, much simpler, is more typical layout art . . . perhaps better.

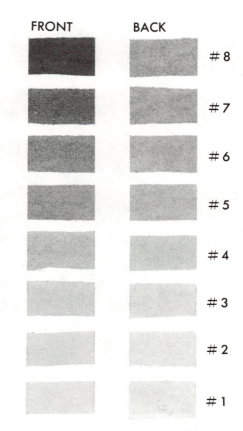

FRONT   BACK

#8
#7
#6
#5
#4
#3
#2
#1

#9 is so close to black it is seldom used.

TRANSPARENCY

The accepted markers for black-and-white lay-outs are the cool greys from #1 through #9. Warm greys are not generally used. All references in this chapter will be to cool greys.

Your success with markers depends also on your choice of paper. On the next six pages I have analyzed the characteristics of typical papers marketed for use with markers. Only by experimenting will you learn which papers suit your personal techniques.

Heavy, Coated Vellum

Drawing rendered with cool grey markers #3 and #6. Heavy black done with semi-dry black broad-tip. Fine lines with felt-tip pen. Background tone #3 cool grey on the back of the paper.

Advantages.   Good transparency. Good effects working on the back. Will take lighter fluid and razor-blade scraping. Good erasures.

Disadvantages.   Very expensive. Not a pure white. Tends to age quickly after going through large copy machines.

#8

#7

#6

#5

#4

#3

#2

#1

TRANSPARENCY

Layout Bond

Drawing rendered with cool grey markers #3 and #6. Right shoulder and top of hair with semi-dry #4. Detail drawing with felt-tip pen.

Advantages. Very inexpensive. Crisp layouts can be achieved.

Disadvantages. Not very transparent. Bleeds badly. Cannot work on the back, except for accidental bleed effect. Will not work with lighter fluid or blade. Erases badly.

Use the lighter markers only. Nos. 7, 8, and 9 all come out nearly black. Very good effects with nearly dry markers.

TRANSPARENCY

Treated Vellum Tracing Paper

Drawing rendered with cool grey markers #1, 4, 6, and 8. Details with felt-tip pen.

Advantages. Very transparent. White. Crisp drawings with strong effects due to whiteness and penetration of dyes.

Disadvantages. Expensive. Dyes do not bleed but penetration is too deep to allow working on the back. Does not work with lighter fluid or razor blade.

TRANSPARENCY

Coated Vellum Tracing Paper

Drawing rendered with cool grey markers #2, 3, and 7. Details with felt-tip pen.

Advantages.   Modest price. Excellent transparency. Nonabsorbent.

Disadvantages.   Though it does not absorb the dyes, it is so thin that markers on the back are almost the same as on the front. Will not take blade, and lighter fluid washes dyes off the paper.

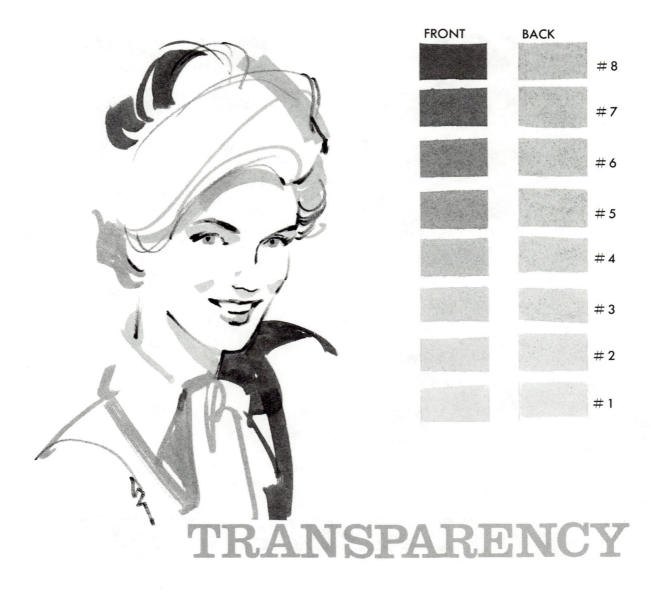

FRONT   BACK

#8
#7
#6
#5
#4
#3
#2
#1

TRANSPARENCY

Light Layout Bond

Drawing rendered with cool grey markers #3, 5, and 7. Details with felt-tip pen.

Advantages. Modest price. Good transparency. White. Fair results from the back.

Disadvantages. Cannot use blade on it.

FRONT   BACK

#8
#7
#6
#5
#4
#3
#2
#1

TRANSPARENCY

Light Layout Bond

Drawing rendered with cool grey markers #1, 3, and 6. Detail drawing with semi-dry felt-tip pen.

Advantages. White. Good transparency.

Disadvantages. Expensive. Though it does not bleed through, it absorbs badly. Cannot work on back. Will not take razor blade.

Marker drawings, rendered with clean, direct strokes, can be very handsome. It is important to accept immediately the fact that *your drawings are layout indications of art to come.* They are not illustrations.

What does this mean in terms of drawing and rendering?

1.   Keep your drawing loose and free, spare and lean. Do your pencils on an underlay and think of the purpose and the action; forget the details and the drawing perfection. The underlay drawing can be messy, dirty. Doesn't matter.

2.   Render with clean, simple strokes. DO NOT TRY TO MODEL. The tones will establish the masses. Let the lines establish the action.

3.   Eliminate as much drawing as possible in the rendering. Let the values of the greys do the work.

The two larger drawings (below, and opposite) were rendered on vellum, the sailboat on bond.

These drawings, while more complex, are again rendered with clean strokes. Verticals play an important part in the structure of both.

The use of the verticals in the water (on right side of the drawing opposite) is logical and creates an action that carries up into the buildings for a powerful unity of composition (the surface lights were scratched in with a razor blade). Less logical but equally as effective is the use of verticals in the grass in front of the tent and in the trees behind. This is not realistic. It is designed to strengthen and bond together the elements of the composition.

The strongest contrasts are all centered around the tent, which is the merchandise . . . the spot

where we want the reader to look. Sky, water, the kids, and the boat are suggested with simple strokes of tone. There is no question about them being there. We just don't want to call attention to them.

The same goes for the distant buildings in the drawing opposite. A few simple tones . . . the mind knows what they are but the eye is drawn to the high-contrast action in the foreground. Again rendered with a minimum of detail. Both drawings are on vellum.

For Your File:

Birch trees are a very handy device to accent outdoor scenes—in appropriate latitudes, of course.

Lighter fluid and tissue can provide the artist with a wide range of new effects from markers. Used with care, they produce subtle tones with a variety of textural surface indications.

This drawing was rendered through the use of several techniques.

The left end of the box was toned in with a #6 marker, then wiped downward onto the table surface with a tissue wet with lighter fluid. Then a shadow was added with a #5. The front side of the box was done the same way, wiping a #3 downward with a #5 shadow.

The lighter fluid can was rendered in the same manner; using darker tones and with more contrasts. To finish the drawing, sharp lines were made with a felt-tip pen.

Below the box, a sheet of typing paper with a heavy coat of #6 on it was wiped left to right onto the layout. The diagonal strokes below the box were added with a #4.

The white outline of the tissue was rendered through the use of a simple frisket (a paper cut to outline the shape of the tissue) and a wiping with a #4.

The tones on these drawings were first filled in
with a #7 marker. They were then wiped with a
tissue soaked in lighter fluid. Then tones were
laid in on top of the smeared area with #3 and
#8 markers (the #8 semi-dry).

The drawing on the left is on vellum, the one on
the right on a coated vellum tracing paper. Note
how much more of the tone wiped out on the
tracing paper.

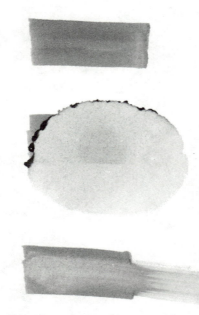

Afterwards, go back and work into the smeared areas as needed. Keep the reworking at a minimum.

The drawing, left, is on coated tracing paper.

The big drawing opposite is a good example of how involvement with this technique can get away from you. This rendering has suddenly decided to try to be an illustration.

Overworked.

By contrast, the drawing below it is spare, crisp, clean. The only use of fluid was to soften a too-heavy tone going diagonally up the mountain.

Lighter fluid can save renderings in that way. Carefully used, you can wipe out an overpowering tone. It won't do a thing on bond paper.

For Your File:

Lighter fluid and tissue are handy to clean finger or palm prints from your layout . . . or marker smears from your hands.

For Your File:

Lighter fluid affects most of the broad-tip (alcohol base) markers, but does not usually touch the felt-tip pens (water base). Experiment.

If you want to go wild and try for exciting accidental effects, pour lighter fluid onto the drawing. By tilting your pad, you can control the flow *somewhat.* You have to be willing to ruin the drawing.

seaways of the modern vikings

For Your File:

A 1″ × 4″ board, drilled with a double row of 1¼″ holes, makes an excellent holder for markers of the short-barrel variety. A board 24 inches long can nicely hold 24 markers. Build it up at each end with a piece of molding so the markers can sit down far enough to stay in the holes. Attach the board at the edge of your drawing board, or wherever it is most convenient for you. A similar board, with smaller holes would accommodate longer, skinnier markers.

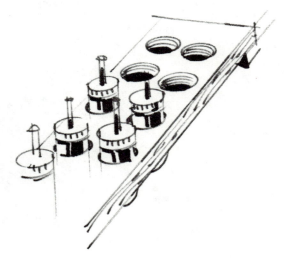

Also very convenient, in addition to tape dispensers, is a number of thin strips cut from masking tape. I keep a bunch of them stuck on the edge of my drawing board. When I'm working with scraps of paper (to save money), the little strips are always there when I need them to tack down an overlay, etc. And they come up much more easily than a wide piece.

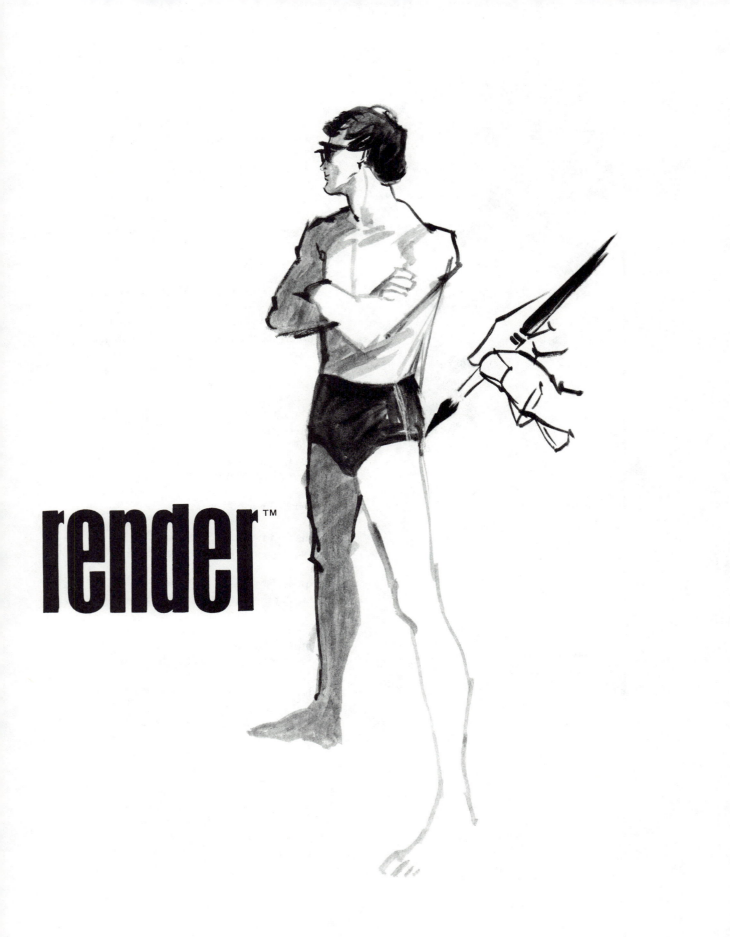

render™

This new medium offers the layout artist the opportunity to paint on layout papers as painters do with watercolor, oil, or acrylic on watercolor paper, canvas, or illustration board. Quick-drying to the touch, about the same as markers, it is like wash in its application (ink or black watercolor wash being the most common medium for black-and-white drawings). Unlike wash, it will not wrinkle even the thinnest tracing paper.

RENDER does not penetrate the paper, although on bond it absorbs slightly (not enough to be seen on the back). There are no such categories as #2, #3, etc., because the dilution of the pigment determines the tone.

Quality of line varies with the brush. The only brush used on all of the drawings in this section was a #3 Winsor Newton sable-tip. It is additionally advantageous that the brush need not be thoroughly cleaned after each use. The remaining pigment will dissolve when next used with no damage to the brush.

RENDER, though dry to the touch almost immediately, remains workable for about 24 hours. Tones can be lightened with the solvent or an eraser, and drawings can be reworked. In areas of heavy, undiluted pigment, it is necessary to blot with a tissue because it will resist drying for extended periods of time.

This disadvantage on the drawing is a definite advantage on the palette, for RENDER will not dry out like oils or acrylics even after months of exposure to air. It may seem to be dry but a touch of the fluid will activate it.

Felt-tip pens can be used for controlled lines in conjunction with RENDER, and broad-tips can be used over it. It works well with a razor blade, as in the drawing opposite in which the broad edge of the blade was used on the ice and the point scratched in the birch trees and even to straighten the corners of the church.

The seascape was painted like a watercolor with a brush loaded with wet pigment. A couple of lines for waves were scratched in with a blade, but essentially it was a wet and juicy rendering. The bottle was rendered with a tissue, with a sheet of typing paper as a mask for straight edges. A felt-tip pen did the lettering and ruled lines, and the dark of the top and label were painted with a brush (the same #3).

Both of these drawings were rendered using good underlays. The tennis player, which is done on bond, was drawn over a careful pencil underlay, while the girl was painted on vellum from a swipe. Notice how much drier the wash effect is on his leg and in the swish of wash on the left, than are the washes on her blouse. This is the major difference in action of RENDER on bond and vellum. All lines on both figures were drawn with the #3 brush. Brush line creates more life in its variety of weights and colors than the felt-tip pen. Only a few felt-tips, used with the side and not the point, can create a line equal to a brush, and then they cannot produce the variety of tones.

RENDER is available by mail order only,
RENDER
1303 Bienville Ave.
Ruston, La. 71270

The drawings here demonstrate the versatility of RENDER—from the quick sketch done with a swipe of the woman in the flowered dress to the indicated illustration of the house. The drawing of the man opposite was not going well, so I wiped half of it out with a tissue and a little fluid, then drew into the grey area and scratched in the highlight of the teeth. An accidental that would be hard to use in a layout, but it worked well.

Back in 1896, a young painter had his first one-man show in Paris. He was approached by the esteemed William Bouguereau, then the most popular painter in town. M. Bouguereau was later quoted by the young painter.

"Why," asked the master, "do you put ideas into your work? With ideas, you annoy your colleagues, your critics, your public . . . NO IDEAS, above all, no ideas."

With this advice in mind, you can be a happy hack for the rest of your life.

THINK!

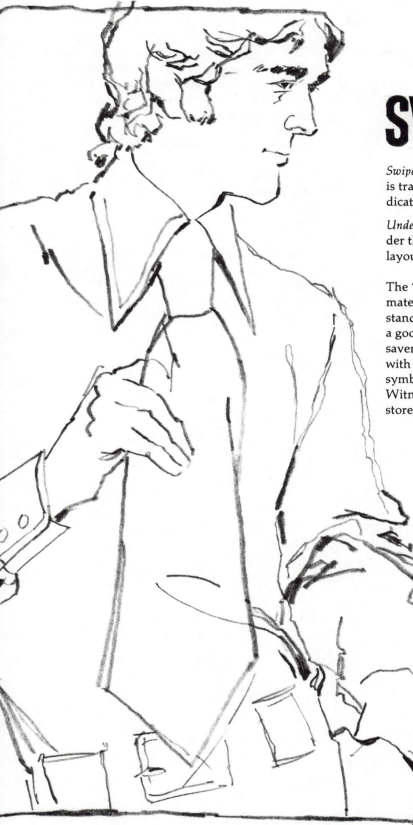

SWIPE

Swipe. A photograph, drawing, or painting that is traced and adapted in the creation of layout indications.

Underlay. Your own drawing that is placed under the layout sheet and used to structure the layout indication.

The "swipe" properly used is an accepted, legitimate tool of the industry. The human body sits, stands, walks in just so many ways, and to have a good file of art on those movements is a time-saver. However, to take the work of an artist with distinctive style, repeat his private drawing symbols, is to steal what is his, and his alone. Witness this gentleman who appeared in a fine store ad of 1972 . . .

... and reappeared in a different fine store ad of 1975. And then, growing a mustache, he reappeared in that same store's ad in 1976! That mustache is a pretty thin disguise, mister. We remember you!

Someone always remembers. Simply because the swipe is such a widely used layout tool, many files (like mine) contain the work of top-drawer illustrators for years back and the possessors of these files are quick to jump on a colleague whose swiping is somewhat less than acceptable.

The name for this kind of creativity is "plagiarism," plain and simple. It is the theft of another's thinking, another's style, another's skills. Study how to adapt and learn from others. Don't steal.

90

The cause of plagiarism in retail advertising is largely economic. The days of models for the fashion artists are long gone. Swipes have replaced them, except in the New York stores where top-quality free-lance artists create new images every week. The layout artist uses a swipe for speed and then, unfortunately, the swipe is passed on to the fashion artist. Because the swipe fits the layout so beautifully, the artist proceeds to use it . . . verbatim.

This does not pertain to fashion art alone. I once had a student designing a book jacket for *The Conquistadors*, a book concerning Spanish conquerors in the New World; his layout showed tepees in the background. The swipe had been adapted from a drawing of General Custer at an Indian camp, the costumes changed to Spanish and Incan, but the tepees somehow stayed!

Here is a drawing that has properly used the original swipe. It is the same pose but not the same man, not the same technique, and not the same action. Not even the same garment.

Opposite is a layout rendering from a swipe in which the garment is essentially the same and the model resembles the original. The rendering legitimatizes it. It has become an entirely new drawing.

Here are four tracings from illustrations in a
1960s ad for the liner *United States* with four renderings that demonstrate proper swiping.

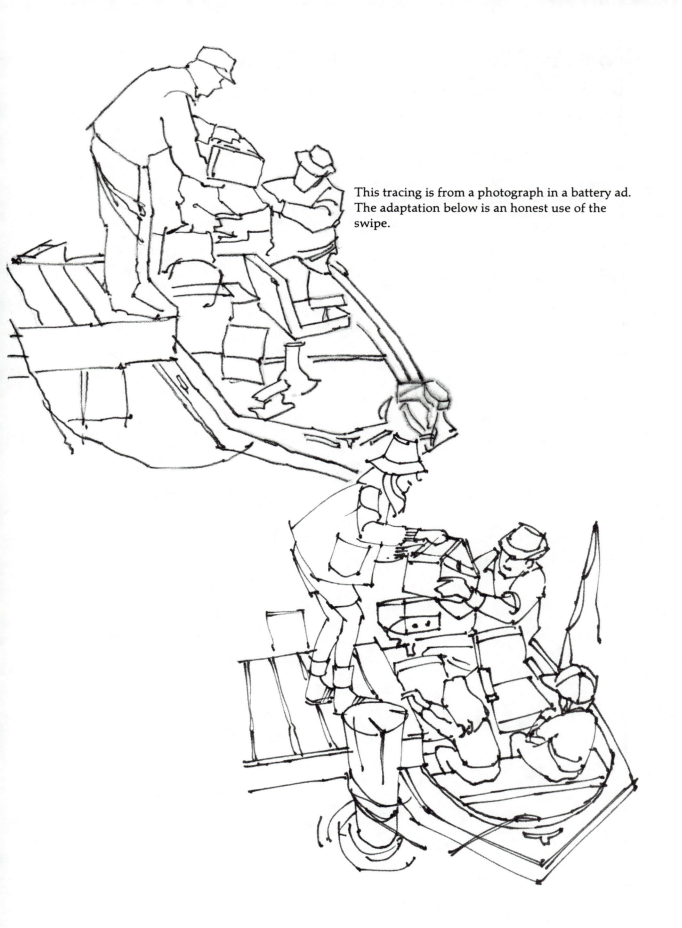

This tracing is from a photograph in a battery ad. The adaptation below is an honest use of the swipe.

UNDERLAYS

The Underlay Drawing

The importance of the underlay drawing cannot be overstressed. With it, you solve your problems of action, composition, etc., on a *separate* sheet of paper, which can be placed under your layout sheet. That is why layout paper is transparent. It is the basis for crisp shorthand rendering . . . and it is the great drawing time-saver.

If your rendering goes sour, move your underlay and start over. If the rendering is done on the drawing and it goes sour, start the whole thing over.

When the rendering looks complete, you can stop even though the underlay may have a lot more drawing on it. Example: the drawings of the man and woman on the right (first rough and final underlay) have much more going on in them than does the rendering.

The tracing from a photo of the man with the teapot has been altered in the underlay drawing to bring his right arm forward, twist his body and push the left arm back. The final rendering would further accentuate this action. This is almost impossible to accomplish in one drawing in a reasonable amount of time.

The underlay drawing shown below, made from the rough drawing at the left, was used for all the ladies' heads that have appeared in this book.

DO NOT DRAW ON YOUR LAYOUT!!

In the May 16, 1977 issue of *Advertising Age, the* newspaper of the advertising industry, there appears a small reproduction of a 1977 advertisement with a headline that reads:

Down from Canada came tales of a wonderful suit!

Very intriguing, good copy—but next to it appears a *1924* advertisement for Canada Dry Gingerale. Guess what the headline said, fifty-three years earlier? You're right—

Down from Canada came tales of a wonderful beverage.

say it better
with the right line

Like the balances of positive and negative space, the presence and absence of lines create definition, action, and direction in layout drawing. A few well-placed lines of the correct "personality" will convey your message to your audience as clearly as the dots and dashes of Morse code to a telegrapher or the notes on a clef to a musician.

Communication is our business, simplicity is our byword. Authoritative lines, simply stroked, are vital. The little man above is not experiencing the impossible. Good lines pay off.

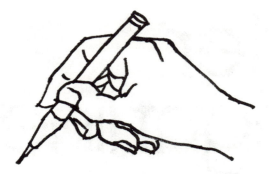

A writing grip produced this dull quality of line drawing.

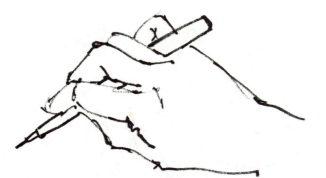

These drawings resulted from this grip.

try a new grip

Your drawing grip should differ from your writing: it should utilize the side of the drawing tool as well as the tip, and allow freedom of hand motion even while a firm grasp is maintained. You can quickly shift back to your writing grip for detailing. Pictured here is a grip in which the weight of the hand rides on the little finger (bent or extended) instead of the palm, thus minimizing the resistance to motion and producing controlled freedom of lines of varying weights and thicknesses. It is particularly effective with pencil and those felt-tip pens that have long points.

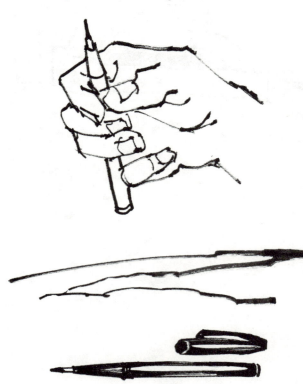

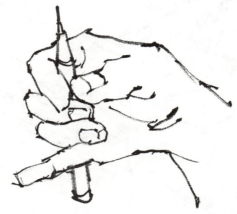

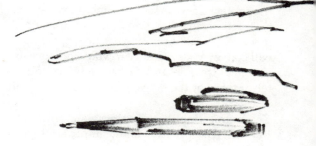

Felt-tip pen

Semi-dry felt-tip pen

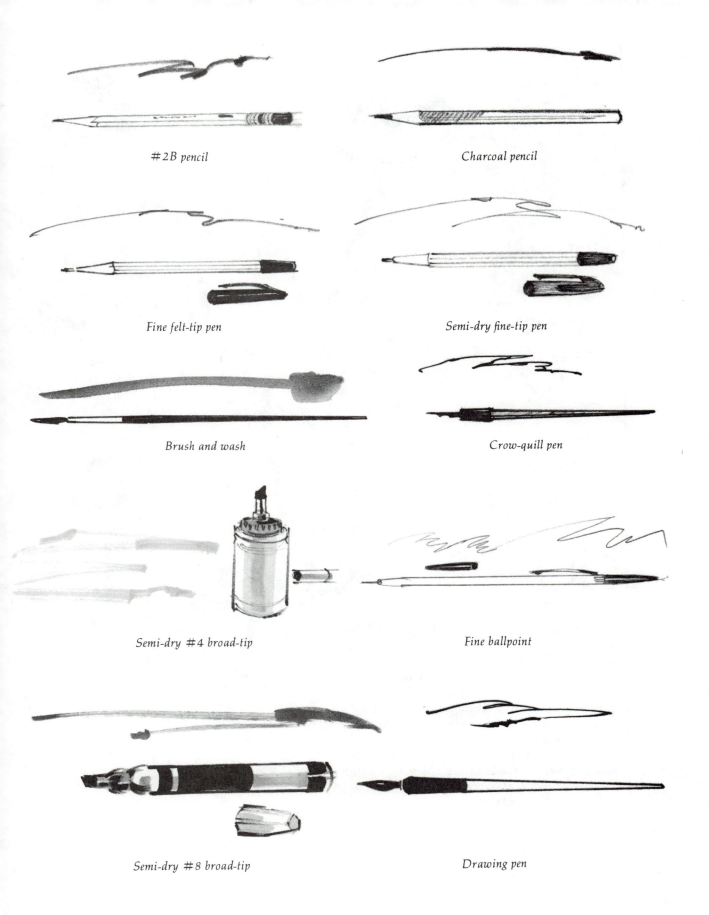

#2B pencil

Charcoal pencil

Fine felt-tip pen

Semi-dry fine-tip pen

Brush and wash

Crow-quill pen

Semi-dry #4 broad-tip

Fine ballpoint

Semi-dry #8 broad-tip

Drawing pen

do

Tones establish masses, lines define action. Minimize the lines in your rendering. Put it all down
on the underlay, then eliminate. Note how few
lines were needed to clearly portray the fat man
and his dilemma. The jogger is drawn almost
completely in lines of varying values, with un-
necessary folds and details eliminated. The tones
of the drawing of the girl are clean and flat, with
one tone on coat and face, a darker one on boots
and hair. Very active diagonals and verticals suggest her vibrancy, as opposed to the horizontal
curving lines of the fat man.

don't

Don't try to model with tones. Compare this poor, muddied drawing (left) with the one on the opposite page. This may appear to be a gross exaggeration. It is not. It happens almost every time a layout artist tries to model with markers. DON'T use tone lines over black lines. Such an attempt to model folds will not work and produces the same muddied result. Suggest folds with line over clean tone. DON'T fall victim to broken lines, timid lines, or (vice versa) a personal exhibition of your slick facility with lines.

SIMPLICITY SIMPLICITY SIMPLICITY

experiment

The pen-and-ink drawings on this page were used as underlays for comps (layouts which are carried to a high degree of finish: comprehensives). The top rendering, an attempt to show two opposing forces in direct confrontation, uses a wildly jagged line; the cartoon is a controlled and simplified drawing of complex action.

The drawings opposite were done with a quite dry fine felt-tip, the larger one reinforced with tones of semi-dry #4 and #6 broad-tips. Both drawings attempted to depict serenity, repose.

HISTORIC SAVANNAH

For Your File:

Always check the effect of broad-tips when you are using an untested line-maker. Don't wait until your drawing is wrecked!

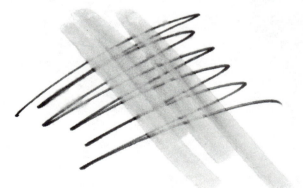

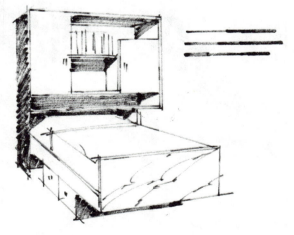

Beat cop

As you experiment with line-makers and line techniques, you'll find yourself becoming more and more intrigued with the opportunities line opens to the imaginative layout artist. Here are a few.

"Beat cop" is an effort to portray the wild, happy activity of the 1890 brownstone-lined streets of New York. Done with a fine felt-tip, it is loosely drawn, with no detail. The glass is a fast felt-tip rendering from a fairly careful underlay. The drawings below were both painted with REN-DER, then scratched with a razor blade to quickly indicate tight scratchboard art.

On this page, a "continuous-line" felt-tip drawing of a TV reporter. Nervous action, clamor are suggested as opposed to the quiet impression given by the rendering of the girl, drawn with a fine ball-point and semi-dry #5 and black broad-tips. The powerful geometrics of the train and plane drawings are relieved by a variation of pressure on the fine felt-tip while ruling in the lines with a triangle.

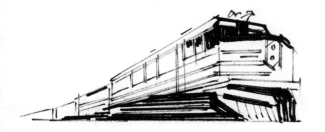

Traditions are beautiful—but to create, not to follow.

—*Motto of Société Anonyme*

When you make a thing it is complicated making it—it is bound to be ugly. But—those who do it after you don't have to worry about making it—so they can make it pretty and so everyone can like it when others make it.

—*Picasso*

The pretty can never be beautiful; the ugly often can.

—*Paul Gauguin*

A short time ago, I received a call at school from an ad agency in a large nearby city asking for the names of recent graduates or students who would be interested in doing some "spec" illustration for them. I told the lady I had two questions to ask.

The first question concerned that tiny word "spec." I never had the opportunity to ask the second question, because she hung up when I gave her my opinion of businesses that want the little guy to take the risk while they stand a chance of gathering the gains.

Never accept speculative jobs (even though everyone who did work free for Hugh Hefner became wealthy when *Playboy* succeeded). Agencies or studios can afford to take the risk of no payment much better than you can.

DRAWING IN SPACE...

With apologies to Hans-Georg Rauch, from whose fantastic drawings I stole the idea, and to you the reader on whom I inflicted it. But consider—isn't it better to be assaulted with an awful pun than to be insulted with the obvious, like a man out in space with a sketch pad? If you have an idea that's way out . . . try it. Who can tell—it might hit the client *and* the reader just the way they want to be hit. At worst, you'll try again.

CHANGE FOCUS

OVERLAP ONE

USE CONTRASTS

DROP ONE

The layout artist who is expert in the profession has taken the time and the effort to acquire and polish the skills necessary to create exciting, sparkling renderings. Unfortunately, he often sees his efforts slowly disintegrate as the layout progresses through the production procedures. A vibrant, integrated design can end up with a dull thud on the printed page. Unhappily, this is a fact of life.

However, a flat, dull layout can never inspire a vibrant finished product. We, the layout artists, must start the project off with the quality of thinking, taut composition, and crisp rendering that will guide the evolution of a successful page in print.

One of the important factors in the creation of layouts that succeed is the introduction of dimension into the renderings. Flat space creates flat drawings, which in turn insure flat layouts. DULL.

On these pages are four very simple ways to introduce space. Though the flower pots are all the same size, differences in placement and rendering bring one forward, push one back. In the drawing, bottom right, the boy's leg has been lengthened from knee to foot. The girl's right leg has been shortened. Where they had been standing flat on the picture plane, they now stand on a plane going back into space. Simply done, and the distortion of the legs does not show.

FOCUS PLUS CONTRASTS

MAYBE OVERLAP CHANGES
THE SCENE TOO MUCH?

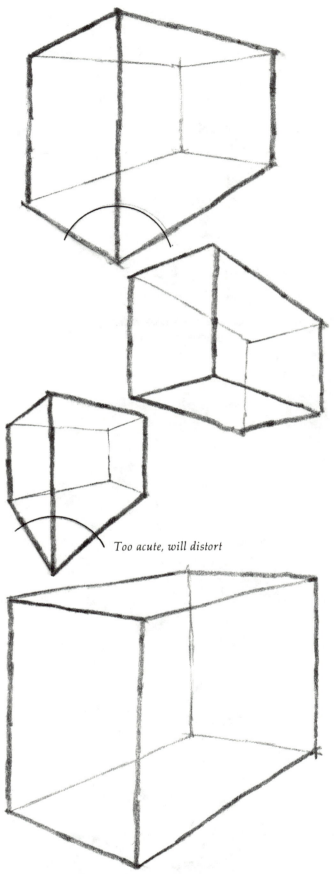

Too acute, will distort

CUBES

Take the time and effort to master "eyeballing" a rectangular area of space. It isn't easy, and you may not see the value of it immediately, but a cube quickly drawn for an underlay allows you to draw difficult objects in space without going into the complexities of linear perspective—and without even seeing the subject.

Avoid cubes in which the angle of the front corner is much under 90 degrees. An acute angle will create objectionable distortions. Once you have mastered the cube, try subdividing it as shown below. These guidelines will carry dimensions all the way through and around the space.

The example opposite demonstrates the value of the subdivided space. The wheels, constructed as boxes and then cylinders, are in perspective, all properly positioned, and with very little effort. The finished underlay drawing is probably not accurate, but it *looks* right.

From a solid underlay, you can render with clean, flat tones with just enough line work to accent details. (See the following pages on cylinders for rendering of tires.)

This same cube has been used on the following page to draw two kitchen scenes. Once you have drawn the space, file it for future use. You'll find many opportunities to use the same cube in a wide range of compositions.

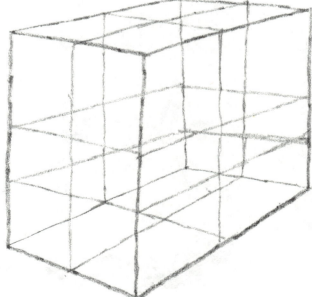

112

114

CYLINDERS

Cylinders are so simple, and so misunderstood. A brief study of their action should solve any problems you may face.

First, the tones of a cylinder go *with the axis* of the cylinder. Don't try to shade around it. Second, when a cylinder is sliced, a series of ellipses occur that will grow deeper as the slices rise above or fall below eye level. Draw the ellipses with a free hand movement; don't draw a concave and a convex line.

Eyeball ellipses above and below eye level. You will soon draw cylinders accurately. Note that the first cylinder below eye level here is hollow. The tones inside go vertically with the axis. The one below is solid; the diagonal strokes establish the solid top.

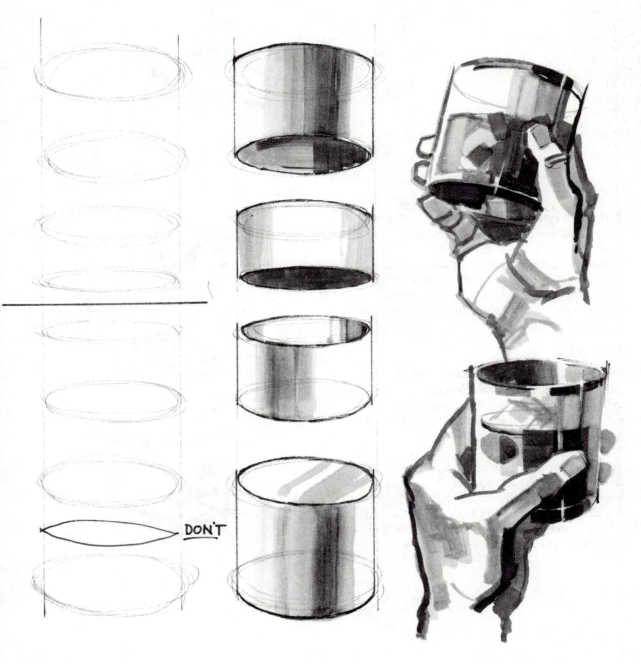

DON'T

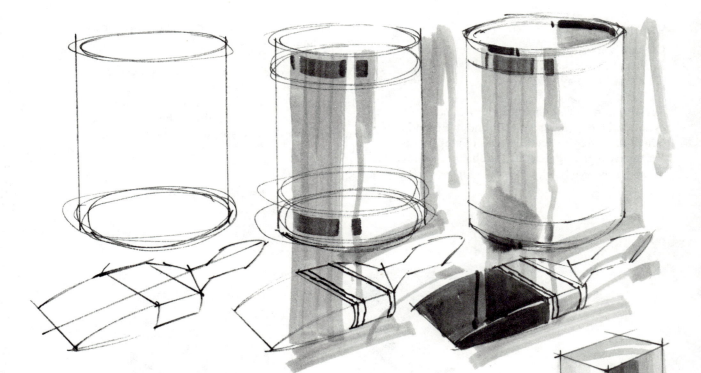

Talk about cylinders . . . we're surrounded by them. Look around, you'll be surprised.

Remember a simple fact of nature . . . lights and shadows fall with the axis of a cylinder. You can draw authoritative cylindrical objects even when faking them. Ignore reflected light or extraneous influences on the action.

For Your File:

On rectangular objects, the darkest shadow occurs directly adjacent to the brightest light. On cylinders, cones, and spheres, the darkest area occurs *within* the shadow and the brightest light occurs *within* the light.

When rendering a cylinder such as the paint can, remember that the lettering, etc., also sits on ellipses equal to the ellipses of a sliced cylinder. In this drawing, I have also used a vertical accent falling from the can down across the bristles of the brush to tie the composition together.

117

CONES

Cones behave like cylinders except that they and their lights and darks narrow at one end. The desk lamp shown consists of a complex series of cones with ellipses of varying size deepening as they rise above eye level. It is important to recognize the action of the ellipses in order to construct a solid drawing (especially if the drawing is imaginary!).

The drawing of a simple cone below has become pretty heavy in the rendering. To re-render would be a matter of minutes.

Starting with a tracing from a photograph that is quite flat, I have deepened the oval area on which the people sit by pulling legs down and pushing the two outer supporting arms higher.

DISTORTION

One of the interests of cubist painting was in the flattening of space. Below is a simplified example. The top drawing clearly designates which rectangles are in front, which in back. The bottom drawing leaves us confused. Is the white a cutout shape lying on top? Are the greys lying on white paper? Etc.

Here is a game based on the same principle. I have made another tracing in which I tried to make all the edges coincidental to each other without overlaps. Arms, legs, backs, all forms meet on a single plane. Through the dark accent, the rendering emphasizes the teacher. Who is sitting in front of whom? Confusing and interesting.

During long hours at the drawing board, experiments like this are fun . . . and you can learn at the same time.

Notes on a train passing through the vast spaces of Texas: clouds don't pile up, they come in layers . . . at you and over you and on out of the picture plane. The closest ones are the brightest white, and crispest darks. Receding clouds become more muted, smaller. The foreground sky, which is at the top of the picture plane, is the brightest blue, and it fades as it recedes (or appears to go downward toward the horizon). The mountains are in muted blue-greys and greyed ochres. Both background and middleground mountains are darkest at their tops with an aura of light below, where they meet dark tones of hills or plains closer to the viewer.

drawing for action

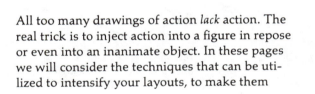

All too many drawings of action *lack* action. The real trick is to inject action into a figure in repose or even into an inanimate object. In these pages we will consider the techniques that can be utilized to intensify your layouts, to make them crackle with energy. Layout drawing offers far greater opportunities for such vitality than does illustration. The shorthand of our techniques presents a continuous invitation to imaginative vigorous action.

folds define actions

It is important to learn about the reasons for folds, and how their behavior, simply stated, can create action in your drawings. Below are the seven basic types of folds.

The top four are active folds. Those are the ones with which we will be primarily concerned. The bottom row contains two folds of repose and one inert. About the only use you will ever have for the inert is in drawing the laundry of the lady who didn't use the right starch.

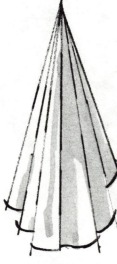

Pipe folds—fall from a single point of support.

Spiral folds—usually tubular with an up or down action.

Zig-Zag folds— occur when a pipe fold is bent.

Half-lock folds—a sharp change in direction of a diaper fold.

Drop folds—irregular folds with dropping feeling.

Diaper folds—fall from two points of support.

Inert folds—like Sunday morning after a rough Saturday night.

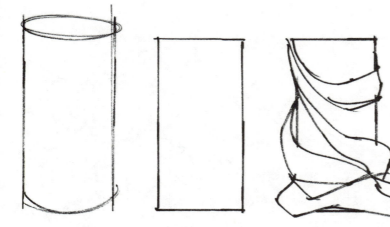

A cylinder without shadows becomes a flat rectangle when viewed at exact eye level. Wrapped in a cloth, it again becomes a cylinder. The folds show it.

1. A flat pair of legs walking fast.

2. Folds bring the right leg forward.

3. Folds bring the left leg forward.

4. Folds make him run with left leg forward.

5. A flat arm.

6. Folds and ellipses push the arm back.

7. Folds and ellipses bend the arm and bring it forward.

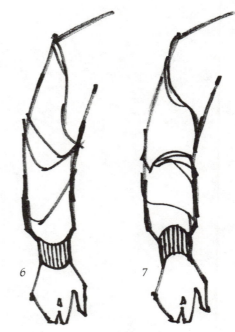

The tracing opposite was adapted from a photograph. The folds are exactly as they were in the photograph.

At the left of the tracing are three roughs of folds for the right arm. The tracing on the bottom shows how the proper folds push the man's arm back into space. The confusing folds on the left arm have been eliminated. The transparent scarf was added to the woman to get rid of the flat, nondimensional look.

Folds of repose fall from *points of support*. Action folds occur at *points of tension*. Keep these facts in mind. Much of this approach to action in layout drawing evolves from it. Left below is a man just waiting for a bus to come along. He is very definitely in repose . . . nearly inert. At the right, he decides to walk instead. Suddenly he becomes a mass of action folds!

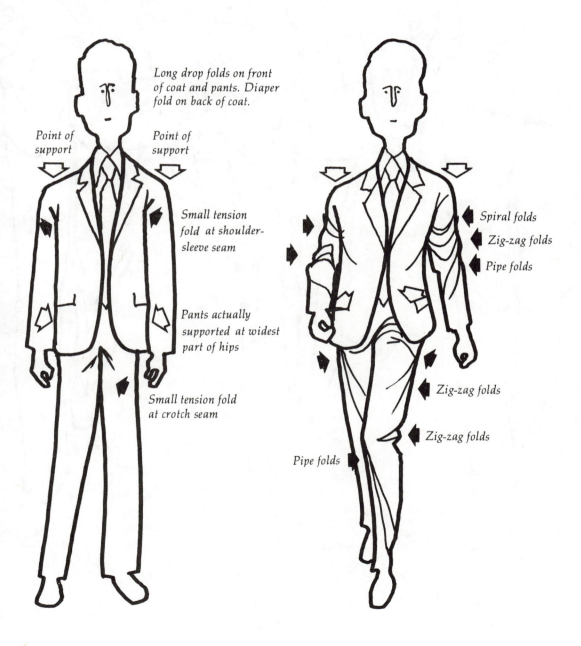

Long drop folds on front of coat and pants. Diaper fold on back of coat.

Point of support

Point of support

Small tension fold at shoulder-sleeve seam

Pants actually supported at widest part of hips

Small tension fold at crotch seam

Spiral folds

Zig-zag folds

Pipe folds

Zig-zag folds

Zig-zag folds

Pipe folds

Here we have a walking man (fashion proportions). The first drawing shows how the hip action opposes the shoulder action. Moving figures always exhibit this opposing action. It's part of our system of balance. Therefore, there is one *high* point of support at the shoulder and hip and one *low* point. They change sides from shoulder to hip.

The next drawing shows all the folds created by the walking action.

The third drawing shows all folds removed from that side of the body in which the *high* point of support occurs. The right arm and right side of the torso are completely flattened. Similarly, the left leg has been flattened.

In the rendering, the effect is heightened when we flatten the plaid on the right side of the coat and shape it with the body on the left side. Additionally, tone has been used on the upper left side as though the light were coming from the right. On the legs, the tones indicate light coming from the left. This "counter-action" not only results in a crisper drawing but adds a twisting action that creates life in the figure.

The idea is not new. It has been known by certain fine artists for centuries. Its adaptation to layout drawing is a natural.

counter-action

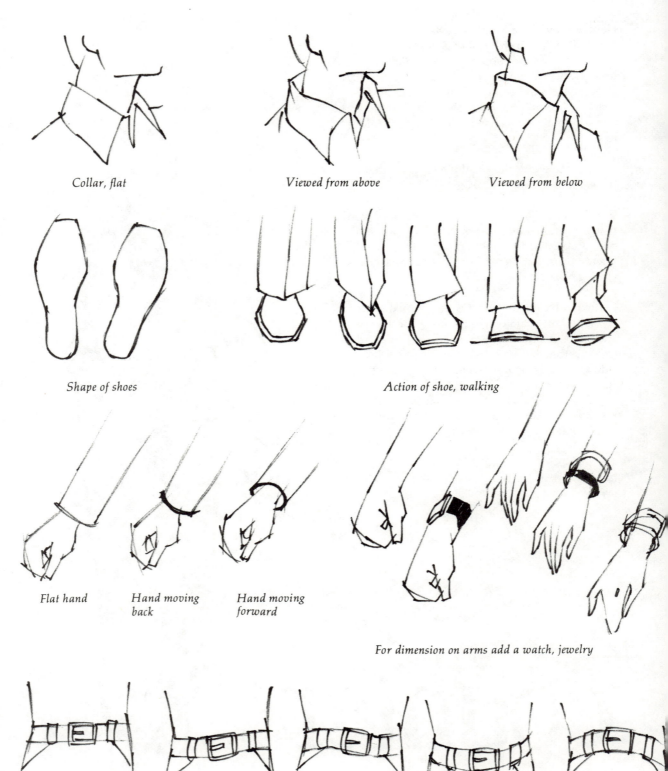

Collar, flat

Viewed from above

Viewed from below

Shape of shoes

Action of shoe, walking

Flat hand

Hand moving back

Hand moving forward

For dimension on arms add a watch, jewelry

Flat belt

Weight on left leg

Weight on right leg

Leaning forward

Leaning backward

soften

the folds and the lines in drawings of women, but use the same principle. Notice the twisting action of the top figure caused by the sudden injection of shadow on the arm only. And the dimensional solidity of the golfer drawn in line without tone to support it.

Throughout these pages I have said that drawings were swiped, stolen, or taken from photographs. Earlier in the book I discussed the proper use of swipes, and I'd like to review for a minute here. The *proper* use of a drawing or photograph as a swipe in layout drawing is perfectly legitimate. It should not be a crutch to carry an artist who cannot draw. It is a necessary time-saving tool which in the long run *can* improve drawing.

The evolution of the drawing on these two pages is typical. The original was a fashion photograph of a girl with two dogs. The first drawing is a tracing in which the garment and hair were changed and one dog was eliminated. The action of the figure was *not* counter: the shoulder and hip were at the same angle because the dog was pulling on the leash.

First, I tried exaggerating that action, left shoulder and left hip both down. It didn't work. Then I switched it completely and raised both the left hip and shoulder. It looked good to me, so I rendered it. The resultant drawing is breezy and fresh, an entirely new action—in fact, an entirely new picture. The important factor is the time involved. On my very best drawing days, I could not possibly have drawn, altered, and rendered the art in even twice the time it took to create this drawing.

Every time you experiment with a drawing traced from a photograph, you learn a little more about the movements of the human figure. When you do choose to draw a figure, it will come quicker and easier, and with increasing vibrancy.

Vincent Van Gogh, *Geranium in a Pot*. An example of the "broken horizon line." Note how the table top changes its height behind the flowers. This works well in layout.

El Greco, *Portrait of Jeronimo de Cavalles*. Dropping an eye, pulling the side of the face forward.

El Greco, *A Lady*. The right side of the face pulled forward and accentuated by the action of the shawl.

Original drawing   *Right eyebrow and eye dropped*   *Right eye pulled around slightly*   *Right side of face pulled around*

Original drawing

Left eye dropped

Right eyebrow dropped

Right eye and brow raised

Right eye and brow raised, nose turned

Right eyebrow raised to see underside

The rendering. Note reverse of the light source

distort

Take a lesson from the masters. Distortion can be fun and can add authority to your drawings. A successful layout artist sits at his board for long hours, turns out quantities of work. If (s)he fails to play with new ideas, and new techniques, (s)he is missing out on one of the most enjoyable sides of the profession. Experiment. Have some fun.

133

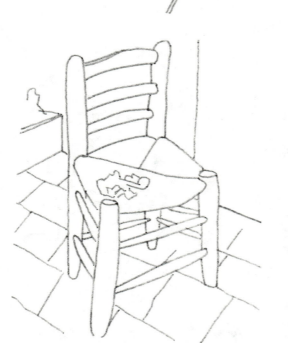

These three fine examples of distortion from Vincent Van Gogh demonstrate clearly how much he made it work for him.

Sand Boat Unloading at Arles, 1888. I have traced only the boat to show how Van Gogh twisted the bow of the boat to suit his purposes. Black accent of the twist is his, not mine.

Les Alyscamps, Arles, 1888. A version of the broken horizon. Notice how the various benches on both sides of the walk (which would naturally be aligned) are not only *not* aligned, but some are also set at angles.

The Chair and the Pipe, 1888. The diagram shows how many different planes Van Gogh chose to inject into this simple object. Then he added even more. He made the tiles on the floor start to slope down and around the chair.

Believe me, I make no pretense of being a Vincent Van Gogh, but I don't mind trying to adapt his principles to my layout drawing (my other drawing too, for that matter).

In this little drawing I have tried it all.

The nose of the boat is twisted around with a strong black line bringing the eye back into the picture area. The positioning of the middle seats, the seating of the children, one edge of their seat, and the lead edge of the dock all employ the broken-horizon principle.

The dock has been tipped up almost to a vertical position. Notice the lack of perspective in the planks. The big posts supporting the dock are in entirely different perspectives.

Is it really worth it? I think so . . . and I have enjoyed playing with the ideas.

Never once have clients given any sign that they detected my games with my layouts, but they bought them.

Study the magnificent El Greco (opposite) and observe: How the *folds* of the right arm bring it around and forward.

How the *folds* of the left arm flatten it from shoulder to elbow.

How the *folds* of the skirt flatten not only the legs but also the big solid chair.

How the floor (as in the Van Gogh) curves down and around the chair. This man is vigorous, ready to pounce.

Above left, a tracing from a swipe and next to it the distorted revision. Observe: Right shoulder up (broken horizon) and right arm flattened to the wrist, where it is squared by the cuff. Right eye brought around slightly. Neck and shoulder squared by collar and exaggerated shoulder seam.

Action of chest accented by open coat . . . Folds of left arm and cuff square the arm. Left leg flattened and pushed back at knee. Crease of right leg continues diagonal of the chest.
This man is vigorous . . . ready to pounce.

Why Bother?

There are probably many artists, both professional and amateur, who will scoff at this concern for drawing, rendering, action, etc. "This is all a lot of nonsense," they'll say. "A layout is only a blueprint for things to come." True, and yet not true. For the artist who spends his hours, his days and nights, at the drawing board doing layouts, the layout is an end in itself. No less than a drawing, a painting, an etching, a lithograph, a serigraph, a book, chemicals in a test tube, a skyscraper, a mathematical formula.

Call it a minor art, call it crass commercialism. It is *our* art, *our* way of life. And it is worth all our efforts, for we belong to one of the largest groups of specialized communicators in the world: a highly competitive brotherhood in which there is no room for slackers.

Rising costs have knocked out all but the hardiest of the magazines. Hundreds of newspapers have died, and direct-mail advertisers are faced with constantly increasing postal rates and production expenses. Financial statistics, hard facts, have zeroed in on the inept. In the marketplace of the seventies and eighties there is no bargain basement for the amateur.

Ours is a very real world, old friend, and to the victor go the spoils. We are not in the layout business for the joy of it (although the joys can be commensurate). Success comes not to the slickest, the most talented, but to the artist who strains his powers . . . who sees, learns, adapts, tries, experiments, grows, reacts . . . creates.

Why bother? Only because it is our life and not to bother is to waste away at a drawing board in a cubicle, among many, many cubicles.

virtually indestructible

FRICTION FIT LID

WEIGHT TESTED GRIP

NO RUST, CHIP, PEEL

12.⁹⁷

FASHION IS THE WORD...

In the world of fashion advertising, *everything* is fashion. Witness these two approaches to advertising a garbage can.

Above, the hardware store or discount house ad. Good, practical promotion of the best features of the merchandise with a strong emphasis on the modest price.

Below, the fashion-minded department store talks color in a romantic way and illustrates to fit—a loose floral background with leaf shadows falling on the side of the can.

Both ads are good. Each speaks to a different audience and knows how to communicate with its customer.

For Your File:

Note how the strong contrasts on the leading edge of the can above denote strength, masculinity, while the soft contrasts below portray femininity.

choose from 4 garden-fresh pastels...

12⁹⁷

GOOD FASHION ARTISTS ARE "PAINTERLY"

These drawings have been swiped rather closely from the work of two superb artists to demonstrate their "painterly" quality. Were these artists working on canvas, the excellence of their painting would be well recognized. Painting for newspaper reproduction, they have to be satisfied with the recognition of their peers. For the layout artist, their work provides a bounty of great swipes.

THE LADIES...

THEY'RE TALL

The two renderings below show how tall fashion ladies are. The figure on the left is of photographic proportions, while the other was swiped from a drawing. They are about the same height, but *look* at their heads. The drawing is over ten heads tall! And that is not as tall as many fashion drawings. Consider the reclining lady on the next page!

THEY'RE AGELESS

Most of them are in their early thirties. Seldom older, seldom much younger. Of course, in an ad aimed at teens, they will be young. Age usually goes along with the price of the merchandise. Ladies in mink coats are usually very tall, handsome sophisticates in their early forties. Naturally, they maintain the figure of a young girl. Designer fashions also provide a showcase for the older woman. Usually forty-ish.

The price of the merchandise usually has a bearing on the height of the ladies also. Here are two renderings from fashion house ads. The tall woman is wearing a very expensive designer suit; the shorter one is enjoying a moderately priced jacket and skirt.

In his twenties *In his thirties* *In his forties*

In his late forties, wearing his $400 suit.

THEIR MEN...

They age, but not like other men. They manage to maintain a rugged go-to-hell attitude. The mouth is firm-set, the eyes squint a little into the sun; like their ladies, they have no personality at all. They are handsome clothes-horses in an ad who must remain completely anonymous.

THEY GROW...
BUT

Not the way other men grow. They grow to meet the needs of their garments.

Wearing work clothes, they grow muscles that strain every seam.

Wearing sport shirts, they grow long powerful torsos and arms.

Wearing slacks, they g of phenomenal length.

The use of folds and lines in men's fashion varies with the garment. The starched look of the dress shirt calls for sharp lines, many straight, while a knit shirt (this one costs more than the one opposite—you can tell by the man wearing it . . . the languor of the pose and the soft lines) calls for more curves.

Similarly, the expensive suit calls for a softer approach. This one is not terribly expensive, but above average. The man does not have the look of very expensive haughteur and the lines in the drawing are too angular for the *very* exclusive suit.

THEIR CHILDREN...

are almost always of normal human proportions. The infants start out four heads tall with a long torso and very short arms and legs. As the child grows, (s)he continues to approach adult proportions.

Fashion children, like their parents, don't do much. Mostly they stand around and look nice in their brand-new clothes. Only in the big nationwide chains do the children actually *do* anything . . . and then it is because the advertiser has a huge market in jeans. In jeans, you have got to do *something.*

Like real people, fashion children go through a very leggy period in their pre-teen years.

For Your File:

Proportions of children's figures are not those of little adults. Starting as babies, about four heads tall with very short arms and legs, the child doubles his head size, triples his torso, quadruples his arm length, and quintuples the length of his legs by maturity.

After maturity, only the nose and ears continue to grow.

The chart gives the proportions of an infant's head as compared to an adult head. The eyes of an adult are usually about in the middle of the head. Note that while the nose and mouth are in roughly the same position in adults and babies, the nose is a tiny button on the baby's face and the eyes are way below the middle.

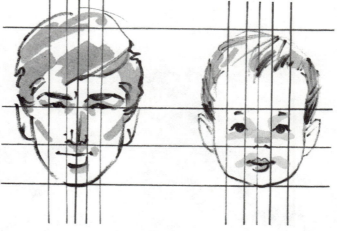

Introducing...
grea~

THEIR HOMES...

are brilliantly clean and uncluttered. No newspapers tossed around, no slippers under the couch. In fact, it is doubtful if the fashion people really live there.

In this rendering, two major actions control the composition—strong darks around the couch, and the verticals of the bookshelves echoed in the verticals rendered in the floor tones. The values diminish at the outer edges, with all the strong contrasts near the center.

All the tones are flat, simple. Many of the lines have been ruled with a triangle.

150

Important in the fashion home is the planting.
The handsome shapes of the leaves, the myriad
variety of planters offer large masses of darks
and accents of lines, dots, and contrasts. Collect
reference on plants. Many layouts could advance
from mediocre to really great if the opportunities
for color and shape offered by plants were
utilized.

For Your File:

Crisp draperies and curtains can be drawn easily
by moving a triangle right to left while going up
and down rapidly with a fine felt-tip pen. South-
paws, reverse the action.

151

THEIR VACATIONS...

are of course exotic. Fashion people usually pick the warmer climates and the oceans. And layout artists have a terrible habit of faking both palm trees and sailboats. For the good of your soul and your future in the business, build a file on these two monsters.

THE NEW CLASSIC MOOD

Here is an example of plants, both real and imagined, creating the mood. The woman's head grows out of the darkest area of the plants and the body is suggested only by a hand and dark glasses.

The rendering is again simple and flat, but the variety of shapes and tones imply a much more complicated rendering. There has been a little wiping with lighter fluid to soften the tone on the top of her head and below her chin.

Excellent books are available to the student of color, and this one has no intent to compete. Instead, here are a few basics for your file:

HUE   is that which we commonly call "color"—the particular identity of red, orange, yellow, etc., around the color wheel.

VALUE   defines the luminosity, or degree of lightness, of the color.

CHROMA   refers to the intensity of the color, the purity, as opposed to the *shade* and tint.

SHADE   is achieved by adding parts of the complementary color or black.

TINT   is attained by adding white.

Warm colors tend to be exciting, happy; cools are calm and serene. Children and teens like bright colors. Men seem to prefer blues, women reds.

I once knew a man in Chicago who had worked in the art department of a large catalog house in the bygone days when all the illustrations were drawn and not photographed. Charlie did the "pencils" (pencil drawings) for men's, women's, and children's figures. Other artists rendered them.

Charlie was paid 25¢ (when 25¢ was real money) for every hand he could hide on the men's figures. He put them in the pockets, behind the backs, sat the figure on them . . . but he hid them, and the renderer came up with another quarter.

A note of warning: when arms or legs break outside your working space, are cut at the bottom of your space, or hide behind another figure or object, be sure the action does not appear at a joint (wrist, elbow, knee, ankle)—the effect is that of an unpleasant amputation.

Color

All layout artists want to show what they can do in color. Color layouts are the most expensive assignments, least accessible to neophytes. The rendering above indicates the use of the ultimate "four-color process" in which the final art, painting, photograph, or drawing appears in full color and is separated on camera into just four colors—magenta, cyan, yellow, and black. Commonly and mistakenly referred to as red, blue, yellow, and black, the *exact* colors represent the closest possible approach to a complete absence of any other colors. When printed, the human eye combines the halftone dots of these four plates to see all the colors of the original. The entire process employs the skills of experts even today when electronic scanners separate colors in one step.

Why, then, have I chosen to render pots and pans as an illustration of layout for four-color process? To emphasize once more the most important word in the language of layout . . .

Simplicity

The color bar, on this page, shows the inks used in 4-color process printing (magenta, cyan, yellow, and black) as they appear on a typical proof sheet.

155

The simplest use of color is in the two-color ad. Black is *always* considered as a color—therefore, two-color means black plus another color. If you have a choice of the second color, be careful to pick one that will (1) be legible when used to print type, (2) allow type to be reversed into it legibly, and (3) allow small type to be overprinted legibly. The red below is an example of a good second color. If there will be halftones of the color, consider the quality of its tints. Many colors are undesirable in 25 or 50 percent tints. Check this on an ink chart at your printer's shop.

Don't overuse or timidly underuse it, as is shown in the thumbnails below. Many clients, and some artists, feel that because they are paying for a second color they should use lots of it. Plan your layout for exciting balances of the colors *and* the white space.

Two colors can also be used as a "duotone" in which the black-and-white art is shot on camera, then re-shot with the screen tipped slightly. When printed, the dots from the two plates will not quite overlap, giving an effect of process color. At right is one way of indicating a duotone with markers. Deep tones of blue and grey were laid in first, then a pale blue and #2 grey were used to lift out and mix the blues and greys. A simple black-and-white rendering with blue on the back would also suffice with the written instruction, "duotone."

Even more than black and white, color layouts tend to make the artist forget about crisp rendering. The results are complex, heavy. At the left is an example of student work in which the artist forgot. The rendering has too many details, such as the face and striped shirt; the artist has forgotten the actions of folds and cylinders (the pants, the tires) and the rendering has evolved as a rather heavy line drawing with colors filled in.

Build your colors as in the unfinished indication above, structuring the strokes, leaving plenty of white accidentals that are strong enough to work for you. Do not get to the blacks until you are well along in the rendering, and *know when to stop*. I realize the admonition gets monotonous, but you are not doing an illustration—you are doing a layout *indication*.

157

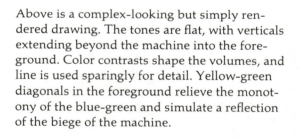

Above is a complex-looking but simply rendered drawing. The tones are flat, with verticals extending beyond the machine into the foreground. Color contrasts shape the volumes, and line is used sparingly for detail. Yellow-green diagonals in the foreground relieve the monotony of the blue-green and simulate a reflection of the biege of the machine.

On the left, a drawing in which lighter fluid was wiped, dripped, and flowed into a marker rendering for high-key effects. Much of the color has been wiped out and the total effort indicates a flood of light and soft delineation of forms. This technique is tricky and should be avoided by the beginner, though it is fun to experiment. Don't work at it—play with it. The best indications will probably be the accidental ones.

The skateboard rendering is another in which marker colors have been laid in full strength and then stroked diagonally with a lighter marker (pink, #1 grey) to lift out much of the original color and give a flowing action. Some areas were even wiped out with a tissue and lighter fluid. Afterward, accents were drawn with a felt-tip pen, solid colors drawn in boldly, and the wheels were re-established with cool greys.

The top drawing on the right (done with render) is highly developed and the one below it left very simple. I would suggest that you be content to leave your renderings clean and flat. Development can lead you quickly into a quagmire. "Happy" development takes a lot of experience, and is not necessarily desirable in every case.

YOU TRULY OWE YOURSELF AN ALASKAN HOLIDAY

These drawings demonstrate the versatility of the new medium, RENDER. Opposite is an indication resembling a painting, yet the simplicity shows in the broad brushwork of the mountain and the sky, which was wiped in flat with a tissue. The whites of the snow were scratched in with the broad side of a razor blade. Heavy darks of firs and water are relieved by the scratched-in whites of birch trees and the shoreline.

On this page are shown loose drawings from swipes with simple, wet brush strokes. The blacks of the man's suit have obviously not been modeled, and no attempt is made to detail the action. Drawing of both the women has been kept to a minimum, emphasizing the value of a good underlay drawing or swipe. The absence of line in the rendering works better than would its presence!

I have not discussed color rendering in pastel, colored pencils, etc. because it is closely akin to black-and-white drawing. Pastels can be used in conjunction with markers for the creation of soft, smooth, blended backgrounds, high-key effects, any mood that essays to be restive and delicate. To spray with fix, not to spray, and when to spray . . . all require experimentation and would be difficult to clarify in this book.

Here, however, is an exciting change-of-pace technique that uses bold and dramatic color with variations of texture—from transparent to impasto—with ease. Starting with a strong underlay, lightly apply acrylics from the tube with the broad edge of a razor blade. Held vertically, the blade will stain the paper with a transparent dye. Tipped, it will apply more pigment for impasto effects. After the colors have dried (except for thick pigments, they dry quickly), draw the details with a felt-tip pen.

BROCHURES AND CAMPAIGNS

There is a definite relationship between the design of a brochure and that of a campaign: the *recognition factor*—the establishment of repeating symbols in a variety of forms. In the layout of a booklet or brochure, these symbols subtly guide the reader from page to page without boring or confusing him or her. All too many brochures do one or the other.

It is advisable to build a file of current brochures. Visit automobile showrooms . . . they are a rich source of expensive graphics. Try the travel agents, catalog desks of the big chain stores. *Fortune* magazine annually lists the annual reports across the country and their sources. Collect brochures whenever they are available.

Many designers and clients tend to tire of a campaign before the public is even aware of it. On the other hand, some campaigns pound away with an iron fist.

Irritating, frustrating . . . effective. Campaign symbols must be strong and of limited variety. Consider the graphics of political campaigns or of the soap, detergent, drain cleaner, etc., manufacturers.

Study the campaigns running in your magazines and newspapers. They will range from the one-week sale at the department stores to long-running successes like cigarette campaigns in the magazines. Look for the recognition factors and study the way they have been used. The quality of the symbolism will vary, of course, but study the campaigns to learn how to build good recognition symbols into your own layouts.

The eight-page layouts shown below are imitations of brochures published by two of the country's largest companies. Both are surprisingly poor in quality of format (overall design).

The layouts on the left depend entirely on beautiful photography (the BIG Photograph again) and excellent color reproduction. The typography is a bore, which in this case may have been intended. The brochure was an annual report and *many* are designed to discourage the reader. After good business years, it would be different.

The brochure on the right has been a layout artist's magic show. He has pulled out every trick in his little black bag and put it on paper. Each of the two-page spreads is handsome in itself, but the reader is forced to hop from one dazzling stimulus to the next totally unrelated visual experience. There is no way for him to settle down and comprehend the message of the brochure.

Somewhere between these extremes is the right path—one that is exciting, but clearly marked, easily followed.

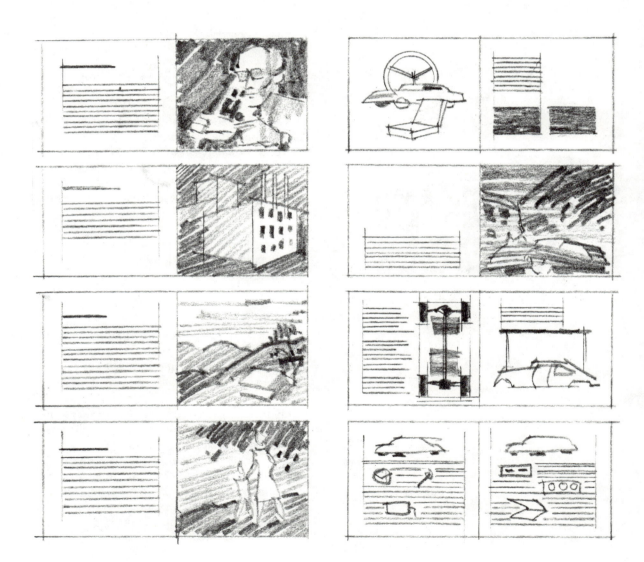

This assignment is a sixteen-page brochure extolling the virtues of a condominium development that has the added feature of solar-heated water and partially solar-heated homes. This feature is, of course, extremely important and will justify the high cost of the condominiums to many buyers. There are also tennis courts and a swimming pool.

To start, I decided that I would use the sun as a recurring element. In a ten-year-old magazine, I found a series of drawings of the sun from Egyptian times to modern: a real find because these spurred new ideas and I had only known a couple of tired sun designs.

Temporarily using a black disc for the sun, I did some very rough thumbnails. I devoted page one to the sun alone. On pages 2 and 3, I decided to show the outside of the condominium in its setting. Pages 4 and 5 were to be devoted to the pool and tennis court. On pages 6 and 7, I returned to the *same layout as pages 2–3* to show an interior scene.

On pages 8 and 9, I planned a closeup of the solar-heating unit with a big change-of-pace drawing of the sun. Change of pace is important—it nudges the reader if he is getting drowsy. On 10 and 11, I *reversed the layout of pages 2 and 3,* planning two illustrations of the benefits of solar heat. Pages 12 and 13 *repeated the layout of 4 and 5,* showing floor plans and an illustration of the woodsy atmosphere of the development.

Finally, on pages 14–15, I *repeated the 2–3 design,* with an idea of showing satisfaction, contentment in the art. On page 16, I had just the logo and address line.

At this point, I cut up the layouts and made a loose dummy. A good idea. Thumbing through a dummy, you will be able to analyze your format, see how it flows, what the immediate changes will be. I noticed that my major repeat layout was sterile, too evenly balanced, dull.

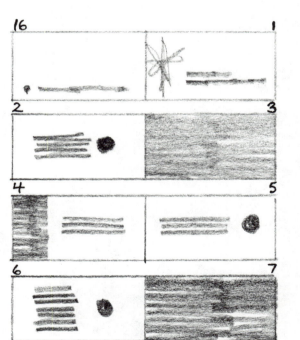

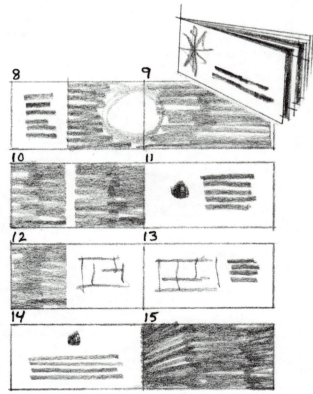

The next set of roughs was slightly more detailed. Illustration ideas came along. I decided to try to take the art areas through from early morning to evening.

This solved a problem that had bothered me on the symbol treatment of the last two spreads. A moonlight illustration eliminated the sun on the last spread, and I liked the little dot on pages 12–13.

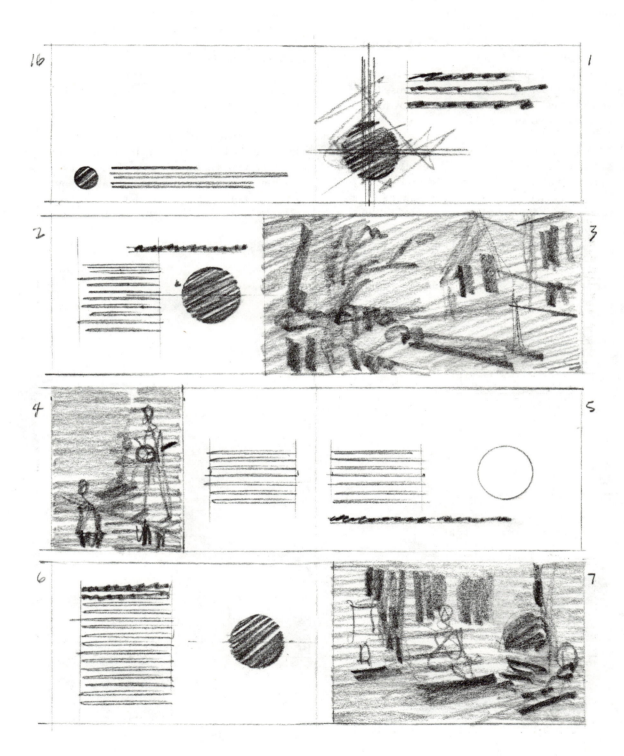

I extended the major illustrations on 2–3, 10–11, and 14–15. Pages 6–7 I left as they were for a change of pace, and immediately decided I didn't like it.

Another element that bothered me was the centered copy and symbol. I decided to drop them both down and allot more white space at the top.

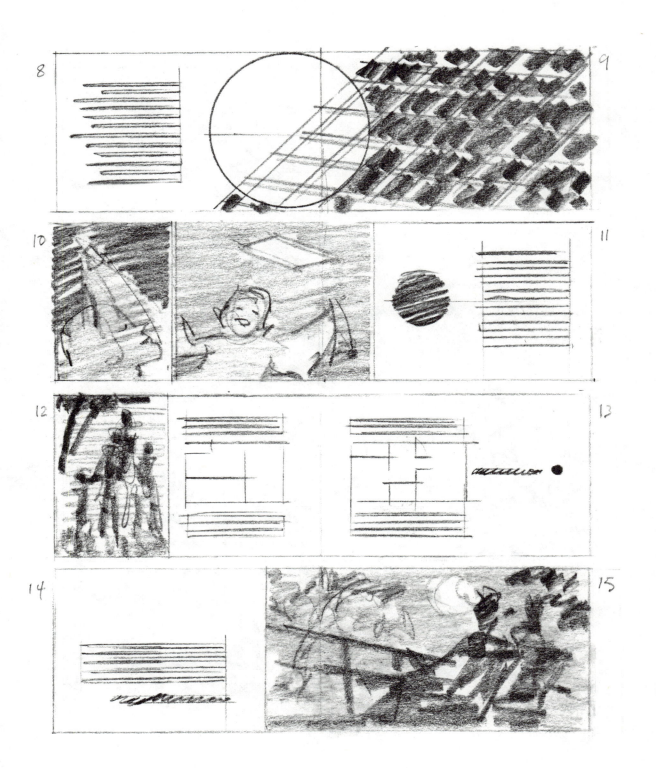

These semi-comped pages pleased me. The adjustments seemed to have done the trick. In many cases this layout would be ready to go into production.

I carried it one step farther because I suspected that my client wasn't able to "read" these layouts. He was willing to pay more now for sure results later.

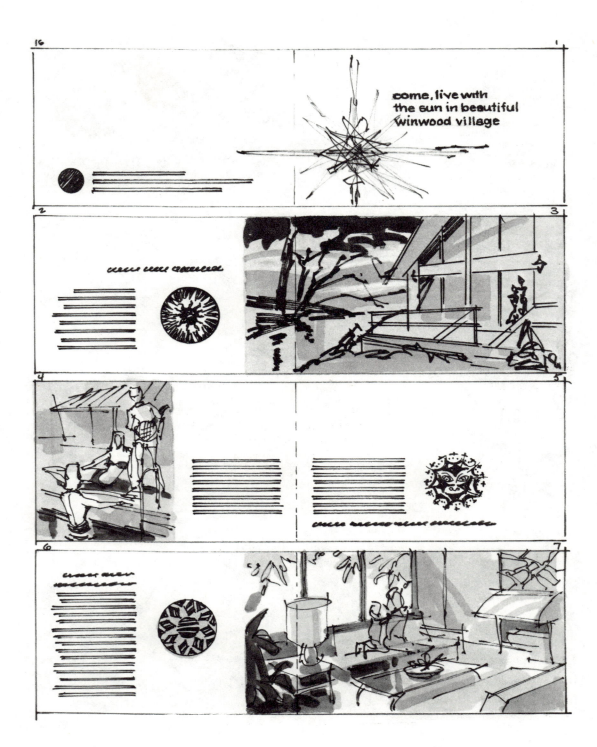

come, live with
the sun in beautiful
winwood village

169

On separate paper (I save all my usable scraps) I drew the underlays and rendered the illustrations. (Again stressing the value of underlays, note how the head of the girl in the shower was tilted further when rendered; this is easy to do with an underlay, hard to do on a drawing.)

The lines of spray were scratched in with a blade on the tones that had been wiped in with a tissue. As always, drawing on the rendering was kept to a minimum.

Final indications in this brochure were done with RENDER.

Now it was time to make a paper dummy with the pages numbered because I had to find out which pages go together for an accurate assembled brochure. The size and shape of a dummy mean nothing—only the correct number of pages is needed. Now I took the dummy apart and found that pages 1 and 16 were backed up by 2 and 15; and 14 and 3 fell together with 4 and 13 on the back. (These are known as *printing spreads*.)

The art on page 3 occupied part of page 2, so I had to cut the finished rendering, placing the large part on the 14–3 spread and the smaller part on the 2–15 spread. Likewise, the art on page 15 had to be cut and positioned.

And so on . . .

For Your File:

If you are a bit sloppy with geometrics (as I am), it is best to draw one outline of a two-page spread and trace it for all the spreads. Small deviations in size can cause big trouble when the assembled layout is trimmed.

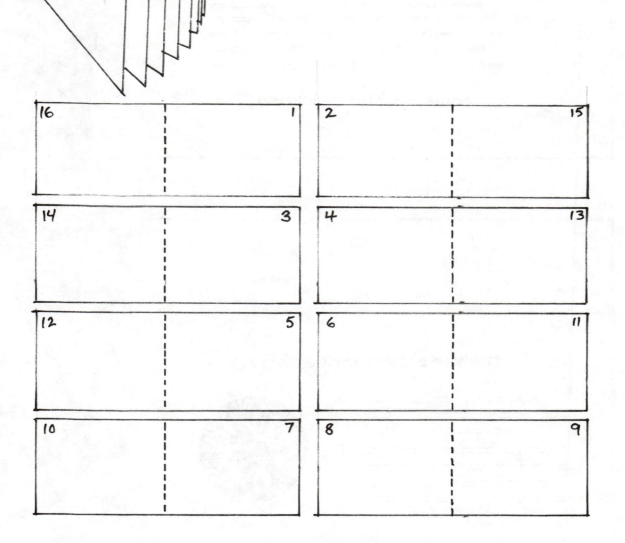

Here are two of the finished layouts ready for assembly. Note that the art extends beyond the edges of the layout. This is to allow for the trim. This *bleed art* must be a bit oversize. These two spreads will be cemented back to back and will closely resemble the final printed brochure in which these four pages would be printed on two sides of the paper. (Before assembling, I would go back and redo the copy block on page 14. The top line is pretty sloppy.)

14

come, visit us tomorrow...

2

this house starts work with the sun

Three adhesives used in assembly, shown below, are spray cement, rubber cement, and wax. Spray cement and wax are used on only one surface for a strong but detachable bond. Rubber cement, on both surfaces (dry-mounted), forms a bond that can only be dissolved with benzol. Rubber cement and benzol both destroy marker tones. Fixative spray will protect them, so be sure to fix any work on the back of layouts.

Trim all the layouts to within about an inch of their edges. Mark the corners and center folds with a felt-tip pen. Cement the back of the first spread and mount on a clean layout sheet. This sheet is used to prevent one side showing through to the other. Trace the corner and center marks on the back. Now, cement this back side and lightly lay a sheet of tracing paper over it, leaving one end of cemented surface exposed for a fraction of an inch. This "slip-sheet" will allow you to position the next spread without the possibility of sticking while you line up the end and center marks (*registers*). *Be sure both spreads are upright.*

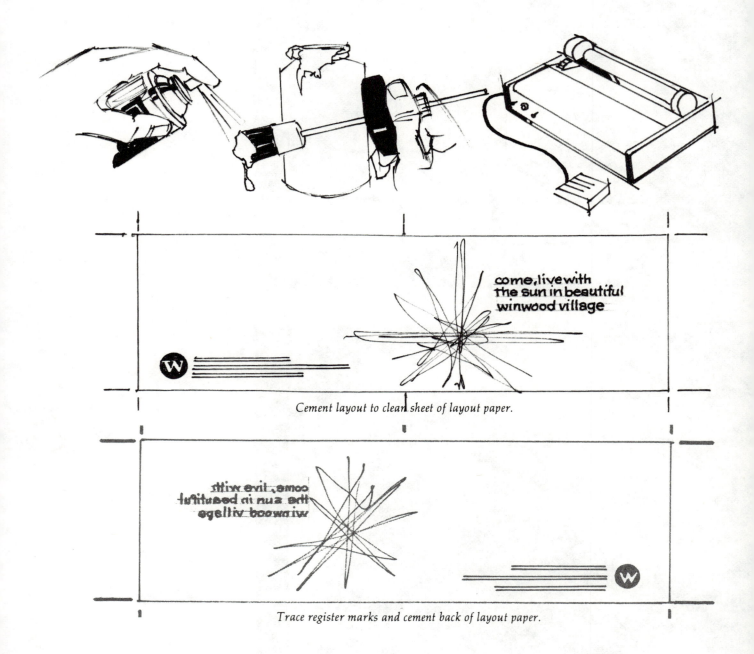

Cement layout to clean sheet of layout paper.

Trace register marks and cement back of layout paper.

174

Press the end of the layout on the exposed cement and gently withdraw the slip-sheet, smoothing the layouts together as you go.

After all the spreads have been assembled, pile them on a piece of cardboard (corrugated is best) in order, with registers aligned. With an opened desk stapler, staple at the fold and bend the staple ends by hand. Fold the brochure and heavily score at the fold with a triangle (cover with a sheet of paper to protect the layout). Finally, trim the three edges of the folded brochure with a blade.

Now, sit back and admire your work!

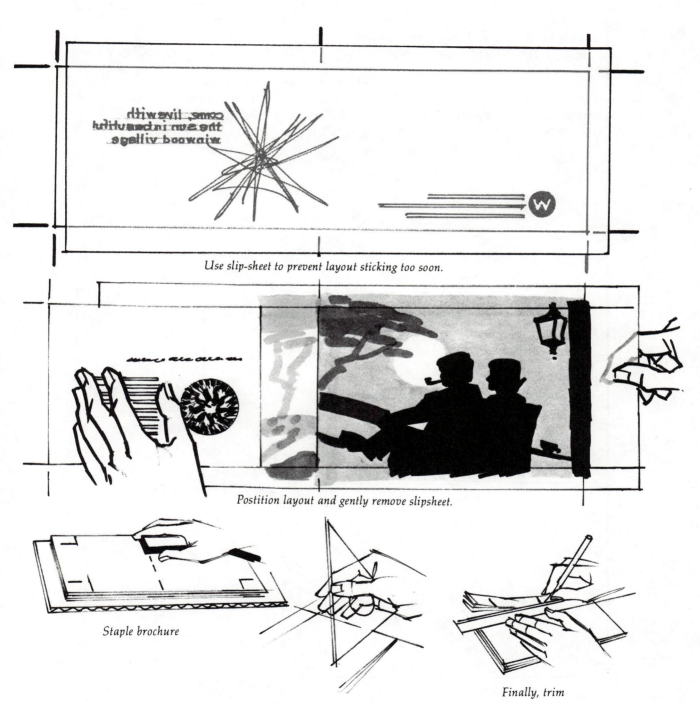

Use slip-sheet to prevent layout sticking too soon.

Postition layout and gently remove slipsheet.

Staple brochure

Score at the fold

Finally, trim

Let's suppose that my client decides to get extra mileage out of the artwork of my brochure and wants to do a direct-mail piece. It is to be 7″ × 12½″ and will fold to 7″ × 3⅛″. He has learned that in order to be economical, the art (color photography) must remain either same size as in the brochure or be enlarged or reduced proportionately. At the most, two different proportions are feasible in the adjustment of existing (or pickup) art to new working dimensions.

Again, I start with a paper dummy. I cut a sheet of paper 7″ × 12½″ and fold it in the middle, then fold it again.

I now open the dummy as a reader would, making note of the order of appearance of the different panels. When I decide which areas

should get the most attention, I number them in order of importance.

At this point I must ask myself several questions. Taking the existing artwork in order of importance: can it be fitted to the areas of importance found on the dummy? Can I use it all the same size by cropping some of it? If not, can I use part of it in the same size and the rest at one other focus (meaning one other camera setting for blowup or reduction)?

It will probably take a bit of juggling, but I have never run into one of these assignments that could not be solved. Sometimes the art can be used all S.S. (same size), but usually one other focus will be necessary.

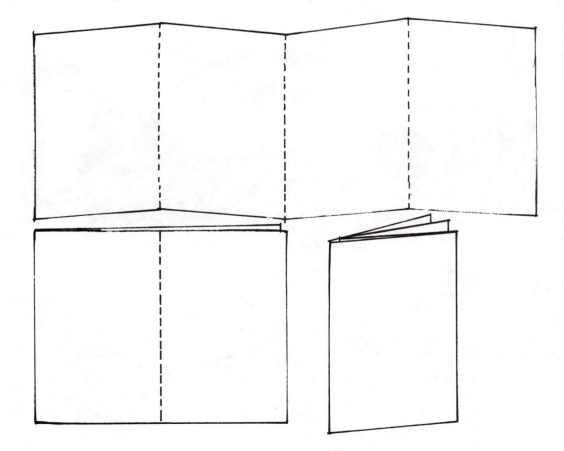

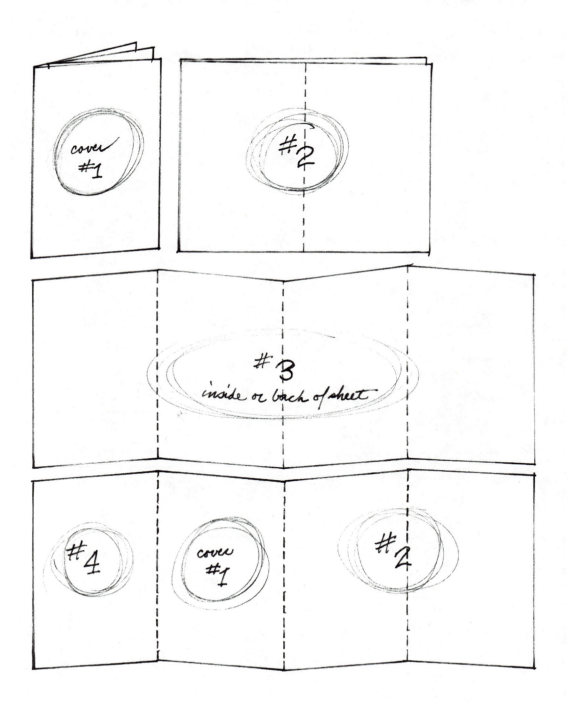

cover
#1

#2

#3
inside or back of sheet

#4

cover
#1

#2

In my layout, I find that I can use the exterior of the house, the solar panel (cropped), and the shower and little girl illustrations (cropped) plus the floor-plan drawings all same size.

I must enlarge the swimming pool and interior scene (cropped) and the cover art.

The relay calls for a different approach, because this is essentially a vertical layout despite its unfolded landscape (horizontal) proportions.

I start with the same cover idea, then pick up the pool and interior on the panels marked 2. At 4 I put the requested reply card and fill with a copy block.

On the inside spread, the floor plans fit nicely above the back side of the reply card. I montage the rest of the spread, cutting into the large illustration of the house with the shower, child, and solar panel.

A rough layout will probably suffice on this project. The client by now should be able to read it. If he needs another comp, he will have to pay for it.

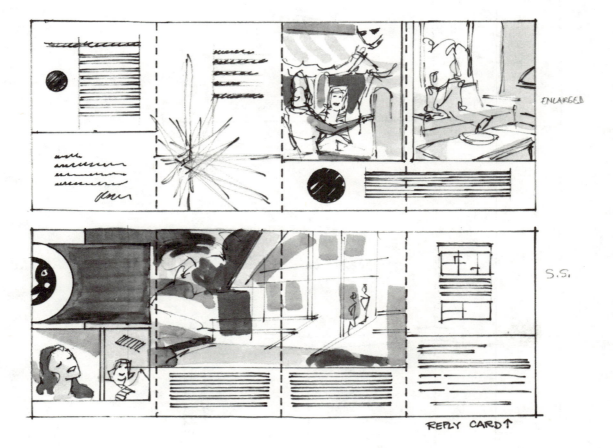

ENLARGED

S.S.

REPLY CARD↑

In order to accurately enlarge or reduce an image, without the cost and time delay of a photostat, the layout artist uses a "lucey" (a term that goes back to the camera lucida, a device through which the viewer looked with one eye to see a traceable enlargement).

Modern opaque enlargers project an image from above or below onto a glass plate, or onto a screen. In each case, the artist traces the image onto a layout sheet. Shown below are several models commonly found in the art studio.

For Your File:

Like our brochure layout, the pages of a book or magazine on the printing press must be arranged so that they will fall in proper order when they are bound. This positioning is called "imposition" and is decided by the binder, based on the requirements of his equipment. The printer must follow through.

When these pages are folded, they are called "signatures" and can contain 4, 8, 16, 32, or even 64 pages. Sometimes they are folded differently for 12, 24, or 48 pages. By folding and numbering a dummy, you can figure out how it works. Books *always* (and most brochures) have even-numbered pages on the left.

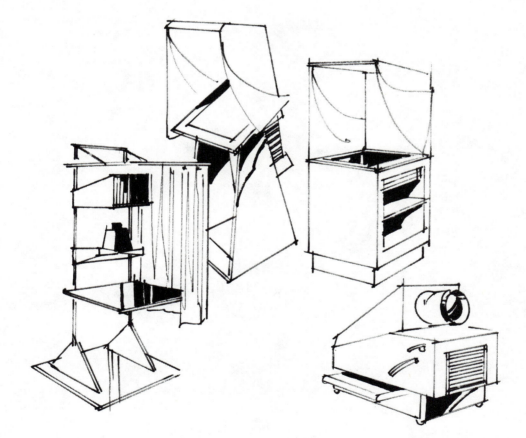

With the decision to publish a direct-mail piece, the client is well on his way into a campaign. He has a brochure and a mailer. Now what can he follow through with? The possibilities are plentiful.

Here are a few, some more practical than others.

T-shirts.　　They could be given away, perhaps in a contest, or they might be sold. Kids don't seem to mind paying for shirts with advertising on them.

Buttons.　　Again, the kids love them.

Billboard advertising.　　Strong emphasis on the identity symbol and very limited copy is a must for a successful billboard; even at 55 MPH, the reader goes by very fast!

Bumper stickers. Maybe the client can induce some of his present residents to sport them.

A newspaper campaign. The client could start with teaser ads for several days before the big ads begin. Again, there should be a strong emphasis on the recognition factors. The big ad should be highly contrasty, fast to tell the reader what's up, and then provide plenty of detail for those who want to read further.

Then a continuing campaign of small follow-up ads to keep the Winwood name in the mind of any prospective buyers. These could be little 10-inch ads or even a 2-inch drop-in like the square ad at the bottom.

Then there's the sandwich board . . .

Billboards, generally referred to as 24-sheet or 30-sheet, can use as few as ten sheets. The 24-sheet board is usually 19′6″ × 8′8″; the 30-sheet 21′7″ by 9′7″, and the bleed board is 22′8″ by 10′5″. Painted displays standard are 48′ by 14′.

Car cards (advertising in buses) are 11 inches deep and can be 14, 21, 28, 42, or 84 inches long. The most popular length is 28 inches. Outside car cards are usually 21 inches deep and can be 27, 36, or 44 inches long. Some are very large—12 feet by 2 feet.

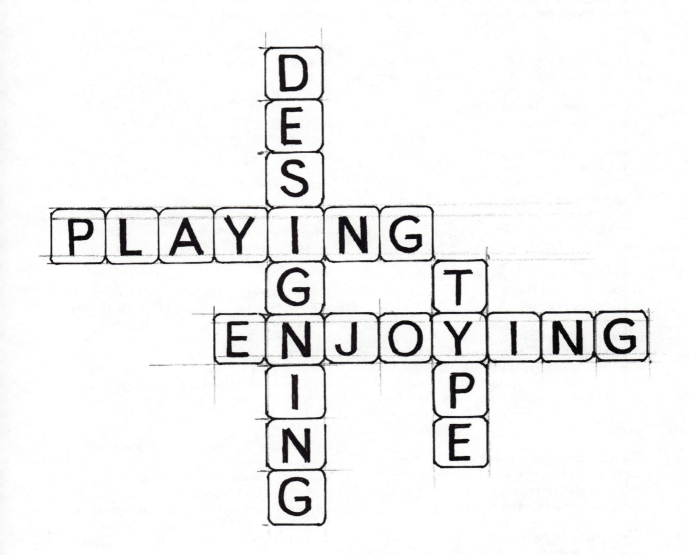

THE POS AND THE NEG...

Typography, employed as an art element in your layouts, can be as enjoyable as or even more enjoyable than the other elements. With type, you start out directly with symbols that have been designed by artists of consummate skill. Where else in a layout do you find this quality of raw material?

With the exception of a large number of modern alphabets—stylistic abortions that have appeared since phototype made the creation of new alphabets inexpensive—type is by itself a thing of beauty.

Your use of a typeface can compliment it or insult it.

Considering type as an abstract art element, what are you seeing? A design of tremendous contrasts. Powerful blacks playing against equally powerful whites. Verticals, horizontals, diagonals, and flowing curves. Thick lines opposing thin lines. Each typeface makes its own positive statement long before the characters are grouped into words.

Every day at your drawing board you will further your skill with type. Attention to the spacing of every headline will help you learn to utilize the positive (black) and negative (white) spaces built into a font of type. (Fonts include all the characters in a particular size of a particular style of type.)

The interplay of positive and negative space cannot be taught to you in a book. You must juggle the letters around under your layout sheet, adjust space, render it, render it again.

The individual design of a company name is called a logotype (logo) or signature (sig). These designs, like trademarks, are usually copyrighted or registered and guarded against imitation or infringement.

Here is an example of the evolution of a logo design as a semi-abstraction. There were quite a few more renderings made, but these are representative. The type style was chosen because it seemed to typify the industry and because the primary use was to be on trucks and vending machines.

At the top are some terribly tricky efforts (not necessarily the earliest). Then the designs begin to calm down. Some look encouraging, some break the word into two separate elements, some just don't satisfy.

At the bottom, the large reverse is a photostatic negative adapted from the word above it on the right. This is one way to comp a logo. First, set the word in *press type* (see definition below). When the spacing looks good, shoot a large negative photostat.

By working on the large photostat with a ruling pen and ink, you can adapt the type to fit the design. (While the ruling pen is not normally a layout tool, it is best for creating the crisp, sharp lines needed in a logo design.) From the adapted negative you can shoot a positive photostat and work on it, if necessary. Or you can paste it up as a comp, or use it as an underlay.

For Your File:

Press type, a trade name now used generically to designate pressure type, is a handy tool consisting of alphabets of various types that are printed on a waxy sheet. When rubbed, they transfer to your layout. For use on comped layouts, they are great—but on most layouts they have a tendency to look overfinished in comparison with the art rendering. They are also costly.

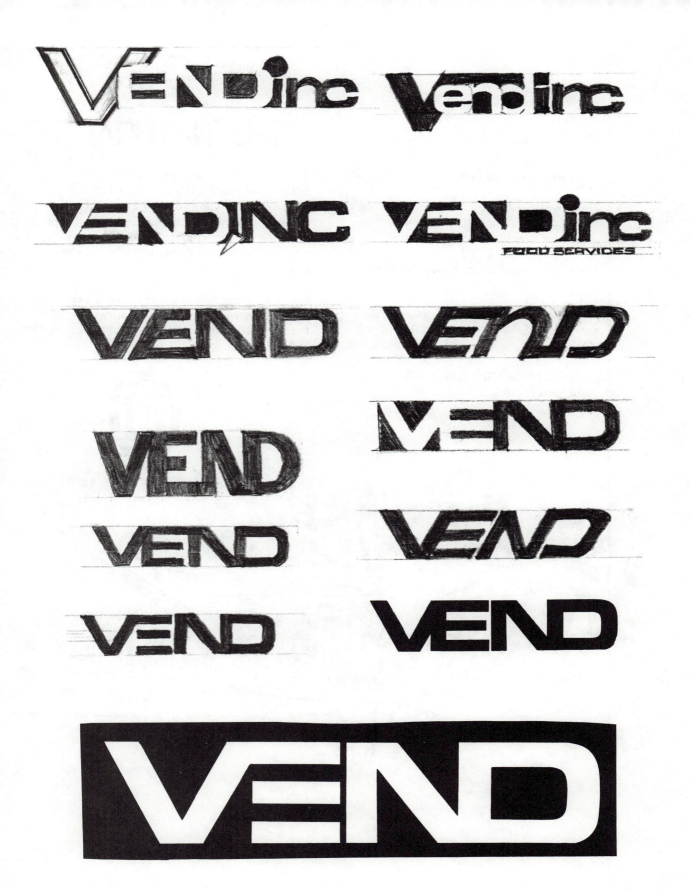

THE "NATURAL"

Logotypes can be grouped in three categories:

1. Those which, either by their letterforms or by abstract designs, symbolize the nature of the group for which they were created.

2. Those which evolve purely as letterform designs.

3. Those whose design has been affected by preconceived notions on the part of the client . . . or the artist.

They can also be classified as "naturals," "average," and "real bears."

This design on these pages is a natural. Starting out with two capital H's in Caslon 540, I immediately saw the columns of an old plantation house (the real estate firm is in Georgia). In the seven roughs at the top which took not over fifteen minutes, the logo evolved; only the shape of the oval was later altered.

Needless to say, this one was a pleasure that has been furthered by the tasteful manner in which the client has continued to use it on his signs and in his advertising.

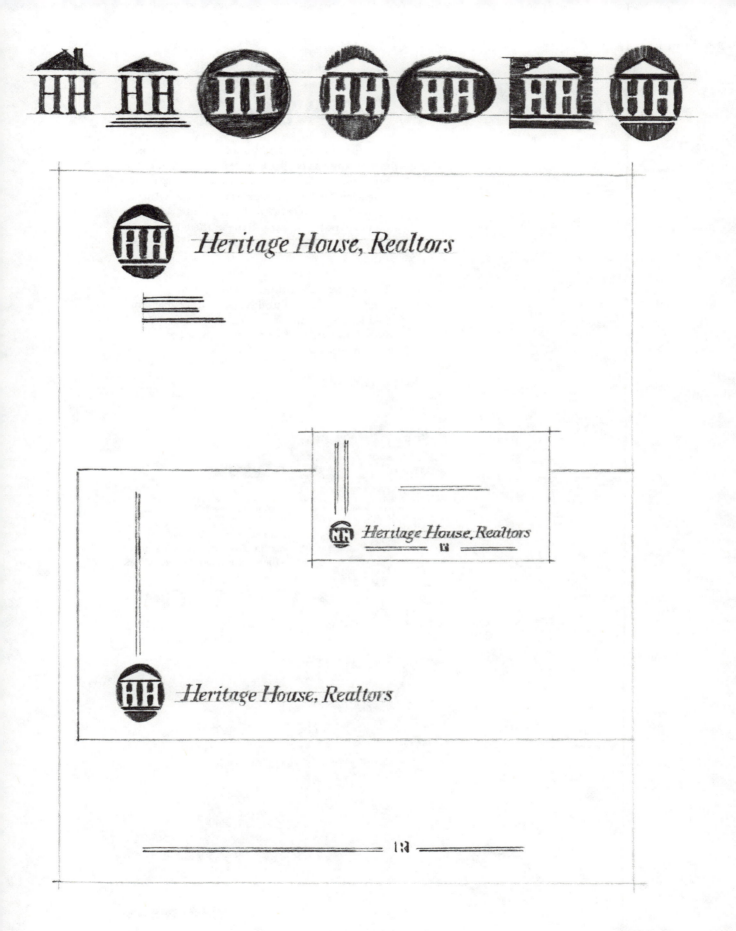

THE AVERAGE...

This logo, also designed for a real estate agent, did not come as easily. Opposite are about half of the roughs. There seemed to be no way to symbolize the design (look at the three awful roughs below!), although at one point I thought that perhaps the square shape at the end of the fifth row might work out as an A-frame symbol (it didn't).

The final result is simple, clean, and well-balanced. I debated about the arrow, but the client liked it, and in retrospect I think it works as more than a trick. It's aggressive, implies action in the company.

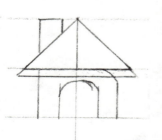

380 CHEROKEE RIDGE
Immaculate 3 bedroom, 2 bath ranch with homemaker kitchen, central air, fireplace, lots of closets. $39,500

WHIT DA
Between Old Lexingto.
Woods on West Side
bedroom, 2 bath white
wooded acres, a large fam.
oversized fireplace. $61,900.

Homes in all Areas with Prices t.
Full-Time Professional Service, Whe..

ATHENS HOMES

ATHENS HOMES

beechwood shopping center
athens, ga. 30601
404 . 353 . 2200

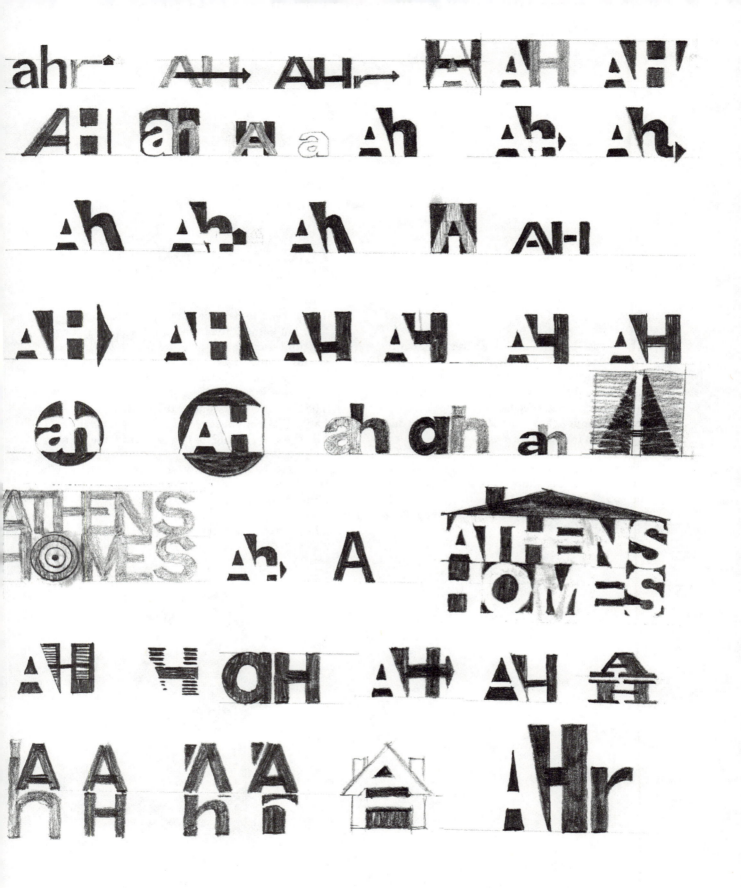

189

THE REAL BEAR...

These will drive a man (or even a woman) to drink!

The client, Aurum Studios, a three-way partnership of jewelry-makers, wanted a logo that could be used as large as a supergraphic on their wall and as small as the hallmark to be stamped on the jewelry. They specified the use of the Greek symbol for gold as the basis on the design and Optima as the typeface.

After a considerable number of roughs (about twice the number shown), I arrived at the large one opposite. It seemed to me to be doubly effective at the time because it also looked like a diamond ring.

It was necessary to make many large renderings. The job was to balance the thin part of the S on the right without the triangle of the A breaking out, find a length for the bottom of the S that would identify the thin leg of the A, balance the A so it would appear to be standing straight.

The first reaction of one of the partners was baffling. I finally realized that the layout was too big; she was reading, or trying to read, the various black shapes instead of the total letters. After she read it correctly, she liked it. Ultimately, the fancy diamond shape was dropped and the circular design was used.

Then I made my big mistake.

SAL

my gal!

ugh!

S+L will get
too small in hallmark

191

In the course of roughing out letterhead designs, I tossed in one with a loose script. *Everybody* wanted script!

For Your File:

When showing designs to clients, use discretion. Don't show too many, even though you might want to impress them with the amount of effort expended on their behalf.

Make your own choices; find the one or two you think are best. Show the client three or four at the most. Make one of them a less successful effort for an easy discard. This will start the decision-making process. (On the other hand, don't show any that are really bad—they might be chosen!)

For Your File:

Trademarks are a more sophisticated form of logotype—often abstract symbols personifying the business of the client. Trademarks do not usually come to the board of a layout artist because they are normally a part of a larger program of design and are assigned to specialized studios. Should such a corporate program come your way, plan to design

1. A logotype, probably a trademark.

2. A designated typographic style for all corporate publications.

3. Letterheads, labels, business papers, etc.

4. Packaging, maybe even product designs.

5. Advertising formats.

5. Signs—everything from the front entrance to the washrooms.

7. Architectural space—the offices, the reception areas, perhaps the plant.

8. Uniforms.

9. Graphics for trucks, cars.

10. In-house and trade-show displays.

11. Probably a manual of graphic standards and requirements for the guidance of all concerned.

546·8826

athens, ga. 30601

p.o. box 164

95 hoyt st.

AURUM STUDIOS LTD. AT THE STATION

AURUM STUDIOS LTD

AURUM STUDIOS LTD. AT THE STATION

AURUM STUDIOS LTD.

AURUM STUDIOS LTD. AT THE STATION
95 hoyt st.   p.o box 164
athens, ga. 30601   404·549·8826

hallmark of craftsmanship and fashion

Aurum Studios Ltd.
AT THE STATION · 95 HOYT STREET · ATHENS GA. 30601 · 404·546·8826

AURUM STUDIOS LTD. AT THE STATION

AT THE STATION · 95 HOYT STREET · P.O BOX 695 · ATHENS, GEORGIA 30601 · PHONE 404·549·8826

193

Over a period of about two weeks, working quite large on a variety of papers with a variety of pencils, pens, and brushes, I wrote over 200 Aurums!

This type of script is not one you can doctor, touch up, and refine. It has to come out all in one piece. It finally started to evolve into a shape that looked pretty good, but always some part of it went bad . . .

Until at last there were three or four that worked overall. In this case, desperately wanting to be through with the whole affair, I matted and acetated three good ones and presented them.

Successfully.

The final choice is shown below.

195

At the same time, I presented layouts of letter-heads and ads employing the logos. It is helpful to the average client to be shown how the logo will look in use.

Life is much simpler when you are dealing with an art director. An A.D. can read your roughs, lead you in the right direction, and help you to polish your work. All the logos shown in this chapter were designed for nonprofessionals.

The designs definitely would have benefited from the cooperative direction of a pro. At the very least, a lot of time could have been saved.

DESIGNERS AND CRAFTSMEN IN METAL

DESIGNERS & CRAFTSMEN IN METAL

AT THE STATION · MONDAY - SATURDAY · 10AM - 10PM

DESIGNERS
AND CRAFTSMEN
IN METAL

designers and craftsmen
in metal

AT THE STATION · PO BOX 164, ATHENS, GE

AT THE STATION · MON - SAT, 10AM - 10PM · 546 - 8826

197

WARNING!

The layout below is an example of a different kind of carelessness. The client had the preconceived idea of a chess piece and motto "It's your move," and I went along with it. For a while I thought that the design had solved it, but I was wrong. It was my duty to the client to show him a better approach. The failure is mine alone.

The design is too complex, the name of the organization too small, and it has never worked. *Simplicity* is the strongest word in our language and this is an example of a layout artist who forgot it.

Stop and think . . . think simple . . . and sell your thinking to your client.

Opposite is a letterhead designed for my daughter and her husband—a gift to them as they started a new business. The layouts were returned to me by mail on the day that I was leaving on vacation, and I hastily farmed it out to a printer for production.

Hastily, wastefully.

The first letter received from my daughter expressed gratitude—with a hesitant criticism that not only was Wood Dale spelled wrong, the address was incomplete.

Exactly as it had been on the layout I had given to the printer!

Note the two printing runs . . .
Note the two invoices.

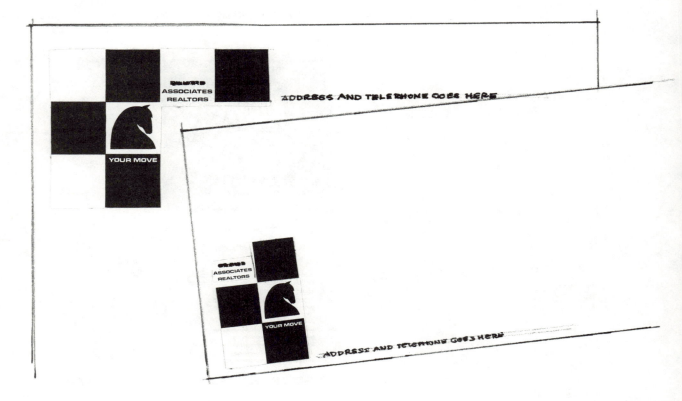

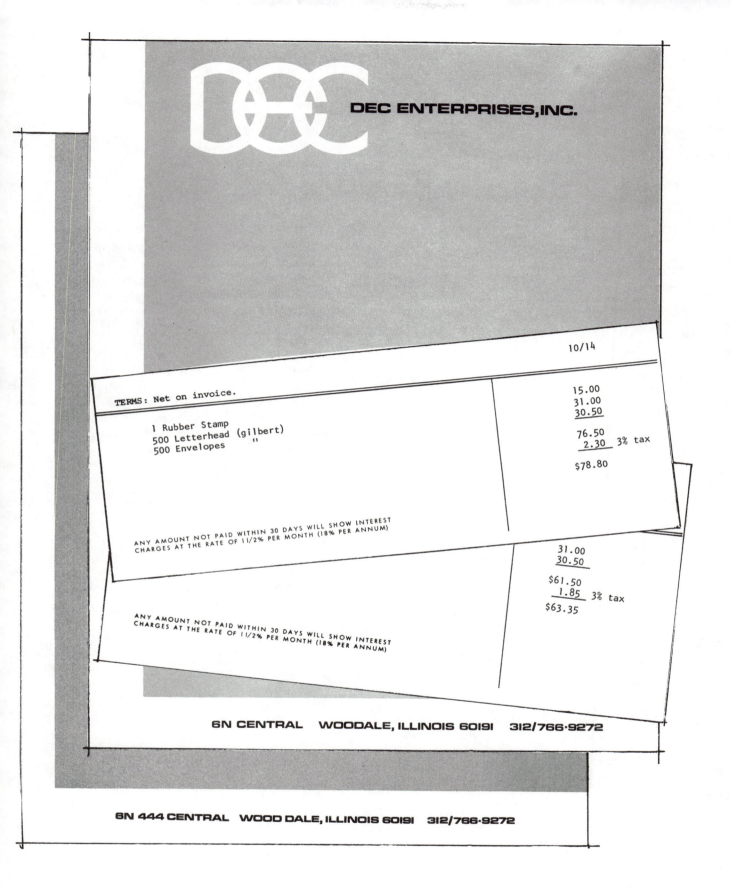

DEC ENTERPRISES,INC.

10/14

TERMS: Net on invoice.

1 Rubber Stamp   15.00
500 Letterhead (gilbert)   31.00
500 Envelopes   "   30.50

76.50
2.30 3% tax

$78.80

ANY AMOUNT NOT PAID WITHIN 30 DAYS WILL SHOW INTEREST
CHARGES AT THE RATE OF 11/2% PER MONTH (18% PER ANNUM)

31.00
30.50

$61.50
1.85 3% tax
$63.35

ANY AMOUNT NOT PAID WITHIN 30 DAYS WILL SHOW INTEREST
CHARGES AT THE RATE OF 11/2% PER MONTH (18% PER ANNUM)

6N CENTRAL   WOODALE, ILLINOIS 60191   312/766·9272

6N 444 CENTRAL   WOOD DALE, ILLINOIS 60191   312/766·9272

199

Two True Stories

Driving us around Mexico City some years ago, our host was obliged to ask directions of a policeman. The policeman gave extended instructions with accompanying arm-waving, pointing, and head-shaking. When our Spanish-speaking host started the car to leave, he summed it all up . . . "He didn't know."

When I quit my job in 1959, after fourteen years in retail advertising, one of my first contacts was an executive of a very large Chicago-based ad agency. After perusing my portfolio, he sat back, gave me a sad, sad appraising look, and launched into a lengthy description of the automobile campaign I should prepare for a saleable portfolio. I was out on the street before I recovered. Fourteen years in retail and the man tells me to design a car campaign . . .

He didn't know, either.

But like the Mexican policeman, he felt obliged to give directions. A common experience when you are seeking employment.

LOOKING
FOR A
JOB

Your Résumé

To cover a great deal of territory in a preliminary fashion, a résumé campaign by mail can be very effective. Particularly so if you create a logo for yourself and design the résumé with care. It is not necessary to spend money on typesetting; a neatly typed outline of you and your abilities will reproduce well and it is worth the very few dollars of cost to have your résumé printed at one of the small letter shops readily available in almost every town.

The design of your résumé can be more important to your future than its content. The community is more interested in your present performance than in your education. Though a degree is not a hindrance, it is not a particular asset compared with the sparkling graphics of your best efforts. The imaginative design of a good résumé can be your introduction to the right art director. Samples shown are those of University of Georgia seniors, with a self-portrait on the front and résumé on the back.

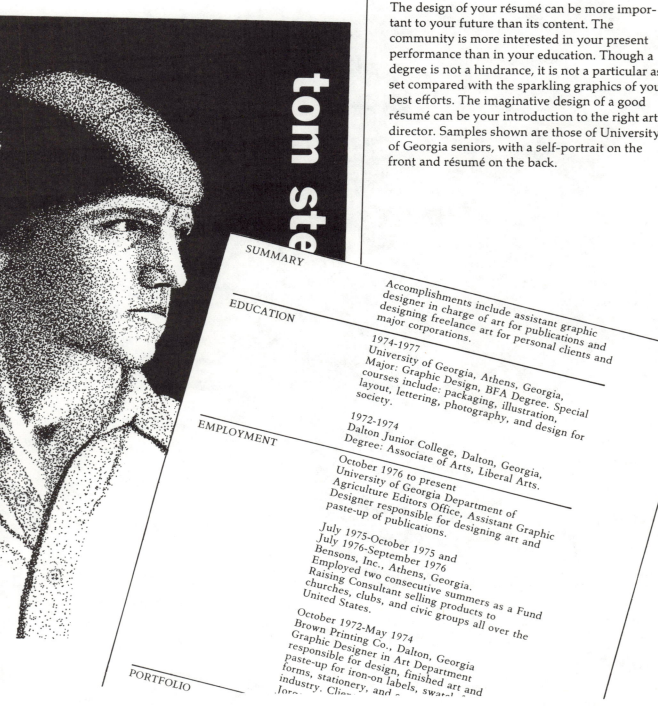

tom ste

SUMMARY

Accomplishments include assistant graphic designer in charge of art for publications and designing freelance art for personal clients and major corporations.

EDUCATION

1974-1977
University of Georgia, Athens, Georgia,
Major: Graphic Design, BFA Degree. Special courses include: packaging, illustration, layout, lettering, photography, and design for society.

1972-1974
Dalton Junior College, Dalton, Georgia,
Degree: Associate of Arts, Liberal Arts.

EMPLOYMENT

October 1976 to present
University of Georgia Department of Agriculture Editors Office, Assistant Graphic Designer responsible for designing art and paste-up of publications.

July 1975-October 1975 and
July 1976-September 1976
Bensons, Inc., Athens, Georgia.
Employed two consecutive summers as a Fund Raising Consultant selling products to churches, clubs, and civic groups all over the United States.

October 1972-May 1974
Brown Printing Co., Dalton, Georgia
Graphic Designer in Art Department responsible for design, finished art and paste-up for iron-on labels, swatch forms, stationery, and ... industry. Clien... Jore...

PORTFOLIO

Your Portfolio

Portfolios are a very definite problem to both the applicant and the Art Director. Many Art Directors are cramped for space in their offices and have difficulty viewing large portfolios of matted work. Not to mention the uncontestable fact that large portfolios are clumsy to carry, impossible to position comfortably in a waiting room or reception area.

Some A.D.'s like to look at slides, others feel that an unprojected slide is like a thumbnail of a postage stamp: too small to allow assessment of its value. Even a small viewer does not solve the problem of scale.

I suggest a medium-sized portfolio with ring-binder. Layouts with white borders make an excellent impression in the plastic sleeves, and the A.D. can turn the pages with no help from the applicant. Include from twelve to fifteen layouts that solve definite problems, *not* revamps of existing ads. If necessary, invent a problem. Remember King Cay? Look back at how that created a legion of approaches. Redesign of existing ads shows only your good taste and says nothing for your problem-solving ability and imagination.

Pounding the Pavement

As you meet Art Directors and Ad Managers, you will receive a bewildering variety of advice. In general, these are great people, but they enjoy talking and (like me) speak from their own experience and are biased toward their own area of expertise. They may criticize your portfolio, suggest changes, probably depress you. Try to absorb what is useful and discard the rest, for when you finally meet the person who has a job opening for you . . . you will be hired. The lectures come from those whose staffs are filled.

Don't be shy and retiring, but do *much* more listening than talking. DO NOT explain your work unless you are asked to, and then keep it short. Art Directors can read your layouts and they generally dislike running commentaries. After all, you claim to communicate in print, so button the lip and let your graphics talk.

You should look as crisp as your work, though business attire is no longer necessary (in my opinion) for a professional appearance. Have a neat, clean, well-groomed appearance; be yourself; smile, and try to be relaxed.

Money

The discussion of money will probably not come up unless there is a job for you. Similarly, if you are seeking free-lance assignments, the fees will probably not be discussed unless you are about to gain a client.

By the time money is mentioned, you may have been able to appraise your interviewer. If you feel you want the job, will you be told honestly what is in the budget for it? Probably the salary will not exult you; pay in our profession is notoriously bad at the start. If you feel confident and excited by the opportunity, take the job.

Start accumulating experience, making contacts, learning the ropes. If the progress on this job is slow, look around quietly. There is a great deal of movement of the troops. Even in large cities, many of the ad people have at one time or another worked for most of the agencies.

The Markets

I mentioned agencies as a starter because all agencies have at least one layout artist. In some cases the artist *is* the agency (and really not a layout artist), while large agencies typically have a number of layout artists, each one handling specific accounts. Art studios are not very likely prospects because layout is not a profitable service for them. Clients do not object to the necessary markup on photography or illustration, but they tend to howl at the costs of layout.

Large department stores have sizable layout staffs; small ones probably have one artist. The pay is rather low, the hours sometimes outrageous, but many artists love retail. It is pleasant to work in the midst of fine merchandise, knowing buyers, getting special treatment when you shop . . . and discounts. Many people consider the security of a large store preferable as opposed to an ad agency, where an account can suddenly evaporate with the consequent disappearance of considerable personnel.

MORE MARKETS

All newspapers offer layout opportunities. Large papers maintain a number of layout people; small ones will probably combine space designing with space selling. Printers often employ a layout artist. Magazines do, of course, and book publishers. Even sign shops, sometimes.

Companies large enough to maintain in-house advertising departments are very good bets. Some of them pay very well, and working conditions are usually excellent. These companies are also a prime source of free-lance work. The presence of a professional Art Director saves the free-lancer a lot of grief . . . and usually assures reasonable pay. Longstanding relationships between free-lancers and ''direct'' clients are common.

The client has confidence in the artist, deadlines will be met; layouts will be imaginative, will tell the story, and will be clear to all who will work with them. The artist has confidence in the client. Information will be well-planned, a quality product will be recognized, responsibility for errors will be (mutually) accepted, and payment for work will be fair and prompt.

All this will add up to a happy, long-term relationship.

SO GET OUT THERE!

Good times or bad, there is a job waiting for you and your talents. When business conditions are cheerful, the Art Director can afford to take a chance on an unknown by stretching the budget a little. When it has all gone sour, your aggressive, imaginative graphic sales ability will be needed.

You have the stuff it takes. Now all you need is a foot in the door and your portfolio can create the opening . . . just wide enough, maybe, for your toes—but you'll have the chance to prove yourself on the job.

And the best of luck!

glossary

All words that are set in *italic* are defined in the glossary.

acetate A transparent cellulose sheet used for *overlays,* or for protecting matted layouts.

adapt To utilize ideas without stealing.

agate lines Vertical measurement of space (there are fourteen agate lines to an inch).

airbrush An instrument used for spray-painting through the use of compressed air and a variety of fine nozzles.

art All *copy* including type, photographs, drawing, etc.

artboards *Camera-ready* copy with all elements in position.

art deco An art style of the twenties and thirties; grew out of *Art Nouveau* style.

art nouveau A highly decorative art style of the late nineteenth century featuring sensuous, flowing techniques.

assemble To put together the *layout* of a brochure as it would appear in print; to put together art elements as camera-ready copy.

asymmetry Off-center balance.

authority Vigorous rendering that asserts authority of thinking.

automatic dropout A method of eliminating *halftone* dots from white areas, on camera, without handwork.

balances The darks and lights, verticals and horizontals, etc.,that make up the design of a layout.

bangtail A form of *self-mailer,* usually an invoice-return envelope which contains an order blank for one piece of merchandise.

bauhaus A school of art at Weimar, Germany which between 1919 and 1930 profoundly affected modern design.

bearing edges In *letterpress* reproduction, the outer extremities of a halftone where pressure is heaviest and ink tends to collect; the reason for avoiding vignettes in designs for newspaper printing.

benzol Solvent and thinner for rubber cement.

big photograph Dominant element of many layouts in recent years.

billboard Most prevalent form of outdoor advertising; commonly called twenty-four-sheet.

bleed Art copy that extends beyond the trim edge of the printed page.

blend To soften tones, one into another.

blind-embossing Producing an uninked raised image on a printing surface.

blowup An enlarged image.

board A cardboard with one surface suitable for drawing or mounting copy; illustration board, mounting board.

body copy The major text of an ad.

body type *Typeface* normally used for body copy; *serif* or *sans serif* with good legibility in small sizes.

bold-face (bf) The heavier form of a *type family.*

bond A form of paper suitable for layout; durable, permanent, usually quite opaque.

book(ing) Assembling a layout in form of final printed *brochure*, etc.

bourges A thin *acetate* sheet with a color coating that can be scratched or washed off with a fluid; used for color *overlays*.

broad-tips The series of markers having broad felt drawing tips.

brochure A booklet, usually twelve pages or more.

broken-horizon Definition of the practice of changing the height of a horizontal line to add life and movement.

bruning A machine for reproduction of large translucent matter, such as layouts.

budget The extra dimension that governs all commercial design; funds available.

c & lc *Caps* and lower-case letters.

camera-ready *Finished art,* ready for reproduction.

camp Trendy, way-out.

campaign A promotion in series form with strong recognition factors.

caps (C) Capital letters.

car cards Bus and subway advertising.

character A letter, numeral, or symbol that takes one space in a line of type.

character count Actual count of the number of *characters* (including spaces between words) in a given amount of type, or manuscript.

charcoal A very soft, black drawing tool in either stick or pencil form.

chop-mark The symbol of a printer specializing in fine art prints (etchings, lithographs, etc.); usually, *blind-embossed.*

chroma What we usually call "color," as in all the colors of the color wheel.

cold type Photographic type.

color In black-and-white layouts, regarding the tonal values of the greys; in two-color, three-color, etc. black plus one, or two, or more colors; otherwise, refers to color as normally considered.

color filters Used on the *copy camera* to separate colors of "full-color" copy (photograph or artwork).

color key Process for obtaining process colors on film by exposure to arc light; overlays of separate films give process color effect.

color process printing *4-color process* separating art into four plates (magenta, *cyan,* yellow, black) which, when printed together, give the effect of all colors; *3-color process* is used mainly for newspaper reproduction, eliminates black plate.

color-separate To reduce full color copy to 4 process colors by using filters on a copy camera or by electronic scanner.

color-spacing Positioning letters of display type so that balances of negative and positive space are pleasing.

column A vertical division of the printed page in newspapers, magazines, books.

column inch One vertical inch of one column.

combination halftone A halftone plate in which both a *halftone* and a *line negative* have been shot and combined to eliminate the halftone dots on solid black areas.

comp A layout carried to an extreme degree of finish; sometimes "high-comps" use finished art and type-set copy; usual comps limit finish to *press-type* and careful *renderings.*

composition *Typesetting;* also, the physical structure of a layout.

condensed Type designs that are horizontally narrower than the usual.

constructovism Russian art movement of early twentieth century which innovated the combination of *typography* and art in design.

continuous-tone Term describes art copy that has a complete range of greys, from black to white.

contrasts Opposing actions of weight, value, and direction for feeling of motion.

co-op (cooperative) Advertising that is partially paid for by a manufacturer, partially by the retailer.

copy The words of the layout; also, all elements of the layout (including type) at the camera stage.

copy camera Large camera on which line and halftone photographs are made of art copy.

copy-heavy Layouts or ads in which copy overpowers art.

counter-action A change of direction, or action of lines, tones, etc., to create interplay between elements of a layout.

cover stock Heavy papers used for the outside pages of brochures, etc.

crisp The light, airy feeling of good rendering.

crop To cut down the size of art by diminishing its extremities rather than by reducing overall focus.

crop-marks Lines outside the edges of new cropped size to indicate cropping without damaging the artwork.

crow-quill Fine-pointed drawing pen.

cubism An intellectual approach to painting, founded by Picasso and Braque, influencing layout design in its employment of *letterforms* and in the flattening of space.

cyan The particular blue used in 4-color process printing.

cut A photoengraved printing plate.

dada An art movement that upset traditional understanding of art; affected layout design by new uses of type in other than rectilinear dimensions.

delete Eliminate.

descenders The parts of a letterform that descend below the body of a letter (p, q, g, j).

direct-mail Advertising matter sent by mail to consumer.

display *Headline* type.

distortion Alteration of art from reality to serve a specific purpose.

double-truck Two-page newspaper ads which cross the *gutter;* usually the center spread of a section that is printed on the same sheet.

dropout A halftone in which no dots fall on white areas.

drymount A type of mounting in which each surface is coated with rubber cement and allowed to dry; when the two surfaces touch one another, a bond is made which can only be separated with benzol.

dummy A blank paper model of a *brochure.*

duotone A two-color reproduction of one-color art made by slightly tipping the halftone screen on the second shot.

dynamics Interaction of elements of a layout to create vibrancy, strength; planned contrasts and balances.

editorial Art and copy matter comprising a publication; as opposed to the advertising matter.

electro A lightweight duplicate of an engraving.

electronic scanner A machine that color-separates artwork automatically in one step.

elements The parts of a layout which make up the whole.

ellipses Shapes resulting when a cylinder is bisected.

em The square of the body of type, often used as an alternate measure to the *pica.*

embossing Creating a raised printed surface by the use of dyes.

extended Type faces that are wider horizontally than normal.

eyeball To draw, in perspective especially, without use of mechanical construction.

face The printing surface of type; also, any particular style of type.

fake process Art that is color-separated by the artist on a series of *overlays.*

faking Indicating art without knowledge of its true form.

family of type All the styles of a particular type design (*roman, italic,* bold-face, etc.)

family resemblance Recurring elements in a series of layouts which establish recognition as a continuing campaign.

farming out Assigning work outside the studio or agency, etc., to a *free-lancer.*

felt-tips Markers, both fine and broad-tip.

finished art *Camera-ready* illustration.

fixative A spray used to protect pencil, pastel, other renderings easily smeared.

flush Vertical alignment (flush left, flush right).

flyer A single-sheet handout, sometimes mailed.

focus A copy-camera setting for specified size of image.

folder An advertising piece consisting of a single sheet, usually printed on both sides, folded two or three times for reading interest and mailing convenience.

font All the styles of one size of one type face.

format The design of a layout, with special emphasis on repeat recognition factors.

4-color process Color separation into four plates—magenta, cyan, yellow, and black—most commonly used for color reproduction.

free forms Extraneous shapes, disconcerting in layouts.

free-lancer A self-employed artist who works as an independent for a number of clients.

french curve A plastic *template* consisting of a variety of curves.

french fold A piece usually folded once horizontally and then once or more vertically to create an attractive folder; printed on only one side, and quite economical.

frisket Paper cutout used to render shapes; especially useful with *pastels,* or markers wiped with tissue.

galley Usually refers to typesetting in rough form, before assembly in position; a hangover from metal type composition.

galley proof An impression pulled from *galley* type.

gestalt Loosely translated, the organization of elements to form a significant whole.

gimmick A trick, tricky idea, device.

glossy A reproduction proof of type; a photograph printed on glossy paper.

golden mean Or Golden Section, a mathematical method of dividing space devised in ancient Greece.

gothic A family of sans serif type faces originally based on scripts of the Gothic period of history.

graphics A confusing term which in some areas refers to printmaking, in others to the printing arts, and herein to the design of the printed page.

gravure An *intaglio* printing method in which the image area is etched into the printing surface, excess ink is wiped from the surface, and only the ink in the etched "wells" reproduces.

grid A geometric pattern used as a basis for design of layouts.

gutter The margin at the binding edge of a page, or inside edge of unbound pages.

hairline The finest line attainable in metal type; usually used as column divider.

halftone Reproduction in which tones have been photographed through a screen, breaking up areas into tiny dots; size of the dots governs darks and lights.

hallmark Originally a stamp on precious metals to signify purity; now a symbol of quality.

hand composition Metal type set by hand in individual letters.

hardbound Or casebound; refers to books having stiff, heavy covers as opposed to paperbacks.

headline The largest *display* type of the ad.

headliner A machine that sets large photographic type.

Held, John, Jr. Artist of the twenties whose adaptation of Art Deco to the American scene of the period had great effect on design.

helvetica The ultimate type design of the *Bauhaus–Swiss–International* schools; beautiful in its simplicity, overused to the point of nausea.

high-key Art that consists of the light tones only.

highlight A halftone in which dots have been dropped from white areas; to emphasize an area of art by dark and light contrast.

hot type Metal type.

hue Gradation of a color.

illusion An image that deceives or misleads the viewer.

illustration A pictorial representation, photograph, painting, drawing, etc., in its completed form as opposed to *indication.*

impasto Type of rendering in which pigment is applied heavily, thick.

imposition Position of pages on printing paper so they will be in order when folded and trimmed.

indication A shorthand representation suggesting the illustration to come.

indicia An area of a printed page left clear for mailing requisites.

intaglio A printing process in which the image is etched or cut into the plate.

integrity The recognition of, and adherence to, physical realities in the design of a layout (i.e., the limitations of typography, photography, etc.).

international style Clean-cut, geometric style largely developed on a grid, based on the style of the Bauhaus school.

isometric A method of drawing in three dimensions in which the scale does not diminish as the object recedes in space.

italic type Those members of a family of type in which the letters slant to the right. Many type families have both roman and italic.

jacket The paper wrapper of a hardbound book; also known as a dust cover.

kerning Shaving the body of a letter (in metal) so that it will fit closer to its neighbor.

keyline Camera-ready indication of art areas by outlines with instructions for the insertion of art matter; also, general reference to the entire camera-ready artboard.

kitsch Bad taste. In this book, kitsch has been included under the umbrella designation of *schlock*.

kneaded eraser Recommended for layout use because of its dust-free cleaning and its easily altered shape.

kromecote A very high-gloss paper excellent for *comp layouts*.

layout The blueprint for construction of vehicles of communication in print.

leading Spacing between lines of copy; name derived from thin strips of lead used with metal type to open space.

legend Descriptive matter under an illustration.

legibility Degree of readability.

letterform The design of individual characters of a typeface.

letterhead Designed writing paper.

letterpress Method of printing in which the image is raised above nonprinting surfaces.

ligature Two letters joined together (æ).

line (line copy) Art that contains no halftones.

linear perspective Mechanical method of establishing perspective by drawing lines to vanishing points, etc.

line conversion Method of translating continuous-tone to line copy on camera.

lines Pencil, pen, brush, etc. lines can be solid black or varying grey, but work in cooperation and in contrast with tones.

linotype Machine for setting *hot type* (metal) line by line.

lithography A printing process based on the fact that oil and water don't mix; water on the plate is repulsed in image areas and ink adheres.

live matter All copy, and those art areas, that are essential to the message.

local (rates) Newspaper space charges to advertisers of the area, as opposed to *national*; rates charged to advertisers in magazines that publish several regional editions compare to "local" rates.

logotype (logo) The *signature of an advertiser; sometimes called a sig.*

lowercase (l.c.) The uncapitalized letters of the alphabet.

low-key Dark in tones.

lucey An instrument that projects an image on a viewing plate, enlarged or reduced.

machine composition Type set on a machine.

magenta The particular red used in 4-color process printing.

makeup The arrangement of copy and white space on a page; a form of layout.

manuscript Typewritten copy.

margins The white areas at the extremities of a printed page, or the white space left at the extremities of an ad.

markers The range of felt-tip drawing tools using alcohol or water-based dyes.

mask To cover an area with paper when laying in a tone.

masking tape A rather heavy paper tape that lifts more easily than scotch tape.

masthead The logo type of a publication.

mat A cardboard, usually white, cut to fit inside a frame with an opening to display artwork.

matrix (mat) The mold from which metal type is cast, or the glass plate containing a *font* of phototype.

matte A nonglossy surface.

Max, Peter An artist whose distinctive symbols were widely imitated in the sixties.

mechanical The final artboard (*keyline, pasteup*).

merchandise The reason for the ad, whether actual physical goods or an intellectual message.

mezzotint A type of *line conversion* with an imposed pattern.

mobility Keeping options open in a design until the last possible moment.

modeling Attempting to create dimension by manipulating tones.

modern type A type face with thin, flat serifs.

modulor Grid system developed by Le Courbusier, the architect.

moiré An undesirable imposed pattern, usually caused by rescreening halftone copy, such as shooting a halftone from a magazine photo.

Mondrian An intellectual painter concerned with asymmetrical divisions of space and color, much maligned by copyists.

monotype   Machines that set type letter by letter.

montage   The combination of images, photo or drawn, into one composite.

morgue   A picture file.

mortices   Holes cut into halftones to accommodate copy.

national (rates)   Charges for space to national advertisers.

negative   Film or paper reproduction in which blacks and whites are reversed.

negative space   White space between and around the images.

newsprint   The inexpensive paper on which newspapers are printed; used for sketching.

offset   Type of lithographic printing in which ink is transferred to a rubber blanket, then to the paper.

old style type   Typeface whose serifs flow into the body of the letter with curves.

opaque   Nontranslucent, light-repelling; to paint out areas on a negative to maintain pure whites in reproduction.

opaque projector   An instrument that projects an image from reflective copy; a *Lucey*.

outline (halftone)   Silhouette; a halftone in which areas have been painted out to form a desired shape, such as around a figure.

ovals   *Templates* containing ovals of varying sizes and degrees.

overlays   Transparent sheets attached to a layout to show alternate designs, or color effects. Also used for instructions regarding art, type etc.

overprint (surprint)   One image overlapping another (as in type over a photograph).

ozalid   A machine that reproduces copies by means of light penetration through the copy onto sensitized paper.

pagination   Numbering pages in consecutive order.

pamphlet   A small brochure, with eight to twelve pages.

parchment   Early writing material made from the skin of goats or sheep; imitated in layout by tones of pastel or markers.

pastels   Soft, dry chalks. Also oil-based . . . not as good for layout purposes.

pasteups   Artboards, mechanicals, etc.

patch   A repair cut into a layout.

pencils   First layout indications; *roughs*.

pentel   A trade name for fine-point markers; name has become generic.

perforating   Punching holes on a line so that paper can easily be torn straight.

photo-engraving (cut)   The plate used in letterpress printing, made by photographic means.

photogram   A photographic print made by exposing sensitized paper with objects placed directly over it to form an image.

photo-retouch   To alter, correct photographs with paint applied with *airbrush* or by hand with brush.

photostat   A less sensitive photographic process used for copying art, either actual size or altered; when photostats are pasted in place on a keyline, they are marked "stat" so that photographer will not use them as copy.

phototypesetter   The modern computerized machine that sets type photographically.

pica   A unit of horizontal measure; 6 to an inch.

picture plane   The point closest to the viewer of a two-dimensional image; the paper, board, or canvas surface from which the image goes back into space.

plagiarism   Outright theft of ideas.

plate   Refers to any printing surface which has been treated so that an image can be imposed; paper, rubber, metal. When inked, the image will transfer to paper.

point   A unit of measure, usually to specify the height of the *body* of type; 12 points to a pica or 72 to an inch (the face of 72-point type may not be an inch in height—the body (in metal) would measure one inch).

positive   Photographically, an image in which blacks and whites are as in reality; positive space refers to the image itself.

poster   A design intended to communicate quickly to viewers at some distance.

press type   Any of several brands of type printed on waxy transparent sheets that will transfer letters to another surface when rubbed.

primary colors   Red, yellow, and blue; all others can be mixed from these colors.

printing spread   Positioning pages of a brochure so that they fall into the proper place when printed and assembled (in a sixteen-page brochure, pages 1 and 16, 2 and 15, etc., must appear together on artboards).

prismacolor   A type of colored pencil currently favored by illustrators; also available in soft pastels (Prismapastel).

process colors   *Magenta, cyan,* yellow, and black— the colors used in *four-color process printing* (three-color eliminates black); can also refer to camera-separated colors other than those above.

proofreading   Reading copy carefully and making necessary corrections in typography.

proofs   *Reproductions* pulled from a plate for final examination before printing, or from type for assembly on artboards.

proportions   Relationship of vertical to horizontal measurements of a space.

psychedelic   A poster style developed in the hippie period of the sixties; derived from the Greek *psyche,* meaning principle of life, soul.

push-pin studios   A strong art force of the sixties and seventies having a profound effect on design in opposition to the *International style.*

read   To understand the shorthand of layout; the judgment of a layout (i.e., "it reads well," or "it doesn't read at all").

reflective copy   Copy that is opaque, usually mounted on *board* (as opposed to transparencies, slides, etc.).

registers   Marks placed outside the image area to assist in positioning printing plates correctly.

RENDER   A new rendering medium ideally adapted to layout; a form of painting that is excellent on lightweight papers.

rendering   The final drawing, or indication, of layout art.

reproduction (repro)   Any copy that is *camera-ready.*

retouch colors   Paints used by photo retouchers.

reverse   To print white on black.

revise   To redo a layout with corrections and alterations; the re-rendered layout.

risers   The parts of a letter that extend above the x-height, or the body of the letter (e.g.,b, d, f, h, k, l, t).

roman type   The vertical form of type, as opposed to *italic.*

rotary   A form of printing from a cylindrical rather than a flat plate; rotogravure, *photo-offset* are most common.

roughs   Preliminary layouts.

rubber cement   Traditional adhesive for cementing art.

rubber type   Type indication that cheats on space needs.

rule   black line used as a divider.

ruler   Measuring instrument; for purposes of layout, ruler should be divided in inches, picas, and agate lines.

sans serif   Typeface without *serifs.*

scale   To increase or decrease a space, keeping the proportions the same.

scanner   Electronic machine that *color-separates* copy automatically.

schlock   Junk, garbage, cheap thinking.

scratchboard   A black-coated drawing surface on which drawings are scratched out in white; in layout, can be imitated with RENDER.

screen   To break up an image into dots.

script   Type that resembles handwriting.

secondary colors   Those achieved by mixing two primary colors.

self-cover   A brochure whose covers are of the same stock as the other pages.

self-mailer   A printed piece that can be mailed without an envelope.

semi-comp   A layout between a *rough* and a *comp;* quite "finished" but not at the stage of *press-type,* etc.

serifs   The cross-strokes at the tops and bottoms of the letters of some type styles.

shade   A variation of color caused by the addition of black or the complementary color.

shading   Attempts at shaping with tone, to be avoided in layout indication.

shooting   Photographing.

shorthand   Indicating through symbols representative of illustration, etc., to come.

show-through   In an assembled brochure, the problem of seeing the backup page through the front; solved by mounting both sides on an additional sheet for opacity.

signs   Everything from a small bulletin board notice to a billboard; quick communication necessary.

silhouette   To white out areas around image to be featured.

slip-sheet   Paper used between two cemented

small caps An alphabet of SMALL CAPITAL LETTERS available in most roman type faces approximately the size of the lowercase letters. Used in combination with larger letters.

solid Type set without leading.

space Areas of the printed page; nonimage areas (white space or negative space).

space rates Charges for use of space for advertising.

spec Speculative. If your client gets paid, you get paid.

spray cement Scotch spray-mount recommended Spray-ment is so quick to adhere that it is hard to position art.

spreads Two facing pages in brochures, facing pages including the gutter in publications.

square halftone Continuous-tone halftone, usually rectangular in shape.

square serif Typeface having serifs of the same weight as the body of the letter, sometimes heavier.

stat A photostat.

step-down A combination of two advertising spaces to form one space that is step-shaped.

stet A proofreader's mark signifying that copy marked for corrections should remain as it was.

strikethrough Penetration of ink so that it shows on back side of the paper.

super realism A school of painting that strives to outdo the realism of the camera.

surrealism A school of art growing out of Freudian psychology that introduced symbols readily adaptable to design.

swash Alternate letters of a face that have curving flourishes.

swipes Art or photography used as a basis for layout indication; a time-saver.

Swiss Also called the *international* school of design.

symbols Elements of graphic communication; the indications of art to come.

symmetry Balanced proportions.

technique Style; methods of rendering.

template A plastic form with holes cut in the shape of circles, ovals, etc., for tracing purposes.

tension The designing of elements to create an interrelationship simulating actual tension.

tertiary colors Colors created by the mixing of two secondary colors.

text Body copy; the typographic message other than headlines.

thumbnail A tiny rough layout showing relationship of lights and darks, very little detail.

tint Obtained by mixing white with a color.

tint block An area of solid color, or of screened percentage of color, usually to be overprinted by another image (type or art).

tissue Refers to tracing paper.

tones Grades of a color from 100 to 0 percent.

tracing paper Very thin, transparent paper; usually nonabsorbent.

trademark A symbol representing a company (usually a manufacturer).

transitional Type styles that incorporate characteristics of both Old Style and Modern faces.

transparent Having the capacity to transmit light to the degree that an image can be clearly seen through it.

transpose (tr.) To change position, such as letters in the wrong position.

triangle Three-sided drawing tool of heavy plastic in the shape of a right-angle triangle with its other two angles either 45 degrees or 60–30 degrees.

trick A device used to convey a slick, usually artificial, message.

trim The final size of a publication after three sides have been trimmed (cut).

trolley A line containing a logotype, address, and miscellaneous information; often runs across the bottom of an ad.

t-square Straight-edged drawing tool with a 90-degree crossbar at the top; on a drawing board or pad, the T-square provides accurate verticals and horizontals.

two-color designs Designs executed in two or more colors are not to be confused with *process color:* the most common use of nonprocess color is the two-color ad—usually black and a second color.

type book A catalog of type faces, either the specific faces available from an individual typographer or a general collection of faces from no particular source; for the purposes of layout, a book with complete alphabets is most useful.

type   The letters and devices used to create words in print.

type face   The special design of an alphabet of type.

type family   All the variations available in a particular typeface.

type high   The standard height of type and letter-press plates (.913″).

type louse   A mythical bug whose extermination is often assigned to apprentices in type shops; probably the same creature that causes misspelling in layout lettering of *display* copy.

typesetting   The translation of manuscript into type following directions set by the layout.

type sheet   A page from a type book (if this book is not loose-leaf, it should be taken to a print shop where the pages can be trimmed loose and three-hole-punched for a very small fee).

typography   The design of display and *body-copy* (text) areas of a layout.

underlay   The preliminary drawing on a separate paper, positioned under the layout sheet as a guide to final rendering; probably the most important drawing device for a layout artist.

underscore   To underline.

unit   Layout elements designed together as a compact entity.

upper-case   Capital letters.

value   The degree of lightness or darkness of a grey or greyed color.

van dyke   A brown-toned photocopy used for proofing purposes.

vellum   A type of paper suitable for layout; the very heavy, coated vellums are the best all-around layout papers—also the most expensive.

velox   A photographic print, already screened, which can be positioned in a *mechanical* and shot as *line copy.*

vignette   A halftone whose edges have been feathered to fade into white; photographs are airbrushed for the effect.

wash   An illustrational technique in black and white using diluted tones of black ink or black watercolor.

watermark   A translucent logotype representing the brand of paper in which it is found.

waxer   Machine that applies a thin coat of wax as an adhesive.

white space   The paper on which no image appears.

widow   A single word, or very short line, left over on the last line of a paragraph.

word space   Space inserted between words of a line.

x-acto knife   A fine, sharp cutting tool.

xerox   A machine producing multiple copies quickly; limited in size of copy.

x height   In type, a vertical dimension equal to the height of the lowercase letters (such as x) without ascenders or descenders.